The Peacemaking Remnant

Essays *and* Historical Documents

Edited by Douglas Morgan

ADVENTIST PEACE FELLOWSHIP
Silver Spring, Maryland

LCCN: 2005928239

ISBN: 0-9770126-0-3

Printed in the United States by
Morris Publishing
3212 East Highway 30
Kearney, NE 68847
1-800-650-7888

Contents

Contributors

Ryan Bell is at the leading edge of the movement among Adventists for authentic discipleship in the midst of post-modern culture. He and his family have recently moved to southern California where he is now pastor of the Hollywood Seventh-day Adventist Church. "Civil Disobedience: Daniel and the Intersection of Allegiances" (Chapter 4) is adapted from the Spectrum Online Sabbath School Commentary for Oct. 30-Nov. 5, 2004 www.spectrummagazine.org.

Charles E. Bradford is author of *Sabbath Roots: The African Connection*, from which Chapter 3 is adapted. His scholarship is recovering a suppressed past, and thereby awakening the church to the magnitude of the possibilities now before it in this new era of *world* Christianity. His four decades of church leadership in official capacities culminated with eleven years as President of the North American Division (1979-1990). In addition to his writing, he continues to empower the people of God by nurturing their gifts in all their diversity, and with electrifying preaching.

Keith A. Burton is President of lifeHERITAGE Ministries (www.lifeheritage.org) and a Facilitating Instructor at the Florida Hospital College of Health Sciences. He holds a Ph.D. in religious and theological studies from Northwestern University and an M.T.S. in New Testament interpretation from Garrett-Evangelical Theological Seminary. He has authored several articles and books, including *The Compassion of the Christ* (Stanborough Press, 2004) and *The Blessing of Ham*, forthcoming from InterVarsity Press (2006). Chapter 5 is drawn from Dr. Burton's 2002 Black History Month Lecture given at Northwestern University.

Kendra Haloviak energizes those to whom she ministers as a teacher and preacher by combining intellectual depth and skillful communication with a fervor both for her subject and for the well-being of each individual. She holds a Ph.D. in New Testament from the Graduate Theological Union and serves on the faculty of the School of

Religion at La Sierra University, Riverside, CA. Chapter 6 is adapted from *Ministry*, July 2004.

Douglas Morgan is director of the Adventist Peace Fellowship, professor of history at Columbia Union College in Takoma Park, MD, and author of *Adventism and the American Republic*. An earlier form of Chapter 8 was given at the Columbia Union College Religion Department's 2003 Keough Lectureship

Zdravko Plantak earned a Ph.D. from the University of London while serving as a pastor. His book, *The Silent Church: Human Rights and Adventist Social Ethics*, was published both in the United Kingdom and the USA. Energy and innovation in academics as well as discipleship and evangelism in contemporary culture mark his leadership as chair of the Department of Religion at Columbia Union College. Chapter 2 is adapted from Dr. Plantak's lectures at the ADRA International Development Conference, 2003.

Ronald Osborn is a co-founder of the Adventist Peace Fellowship and principal author of its statements of Vision and Covenant. He is completing graduate work in international relations at the London School of Economics, and has authored several provocative articles and presentations on political ideologies in the light of radical Christianity. An earlier version of Chapter 7 appeared in *Adventist Today*, November-December 2003.

Charles Scriven continues decades of service to the Adventist community as scholar, pastor, author, editor, teacher, administrator, and — through each capacity — prophetic voice. He is President of Kettering College of Medical Arts in Ohio and of the Association of Adventist Forums. Chapter 1, and the overall title for this book, are taken from his "The Peacemaking Remnant: Dreaming a Grander Dream" in *Spectrum*, Summer 1999.

Preface

This collection of essays and historical documents offers
evidence that "peacemaking" and "remnant" belong
together. Peacemaking names, not just one of many
Christian ideals, but a defining dimension of the biblical
remnant. Making *shalom* (peace) — well-being and wholeness for
the human community that includes but goes beyond
nonviolence — runs like a mighty stream through all of the
particular truths that the Seventh-day Adventist movement has
been called to proclaim.

The first six chapters of this book explore the significance for
peacemaking, in that broad sense, of a biblical theme, symbol, or
doctrine central to the Adventist identity. Each chapter has been
adapted with the author's permission from material already
published or presented. The essays vary in style and mode.
They are brought together here to elicit conversation about
Adventism and peacemaking, rather than as a systematic
treatment of the topic.

For the past two decades the most articulate, informed, and
insistent voice for peacemaking in the Adventist community has
been that of Charles Scriven. His title essay addresses what
Adventists have always aspired to be, even as they struggle over
its meaning — a faithful *remnant*.

Exploring the Adventist vocation through another lens,
Zdravko Plantak looks beyond apocalyptic prophecy to a broad
range of prophets in the Bible for a deepened understanding of
what it means to be a *people of prophecy*.

The Sabbath, we are reminded by Deuteronomy 5, is not only
about creation but also about the Creator's liberating action to
redeem it. In the current phase of his ministry, Charles E.
Bradford is leading the church with pioneering scholarship on
the neglected history of the *seventh-day Sabbath* in the liberation

of peoples of African heritage. For today and for all peoples, that history points to a genuine theology of liberation.

The biblical book of Daniel combines, with prophecies, stories modeling the way of a *true witness* under the pressure of apocalyptic crisis. Ryan Bell reflects on Daniel as a true witness for God's peaceable kingdom amidst the political strife of human empires, and how he managed to act faithfully through both statesmanship and civil disobedience.

Keith Burton disabuses the reader of any notion that biblical peacemaking is about pleasing everybody. The message of peace afflicts the comfortable as well as comforting the afflicted. It confronts those who destroy peace by purveying militarism, poverty, and racism with the announcement of the *hour of God's judgment*.

While the book of Revelation has always been of central significance for Adventists, we have missed much of its power by rushing too quickly past its passages of praise, worship, and glory. Kendra Haloviak, drawing on her doctoral research, shows how this awesome hymnody animates the *blessed hope*.

History honestly interpreted usually brings both dismay and delight. In Chapter 7, Ronald Osborn traces a disturbing decline in Adventist commitment to nonviolence. Yet his essay also inspires by pointing to the possibility of recovering of lost historical treasure. Trends prevailing since the 1930s need not define us. My own essay further explores some evidence of a peacemaking heritage. Then, we provide a selection of historical documents upon which readers may draw in weighing evidence for themselves.

We conclude with information on the publisher of the book, the Adventist Peace Fellowship, and its quest to be part of a faithful remnant's journey toward being "God's partners in peacemaking."

Douglas Morgan
Silver Spring, Maryland
May 2005

> **"And the dragon was wroth with the woman, and went to make war with the remnant of her seed, which keep the commandments of God, and have the testimony of Jesus Christ"**
> **(Revelation 12:17)**

1

The Peacemaking Remnant

Spirituality and Mission for a People of Hope

CHARLES SCRIVEN

"I will teach you the fear of the Lord...seek peace, and pursue it."
--David[1]
"Blessed are the peacemakers, for they will be called the children of God"
--Jesus of Nazareth[2]

"...God works out His purpose through a 'remnant', a minority ready to think and act ahead of the community as a whole, and so keep alive the vision of God's redemptive way."
--G. H. C. Macgregor[3]

Despite a wealth of corrective scholarship, from our own and other writers, the dominant Adventist eschatology continues to see the spiritual life as escape and church mission as talk. End-time believers, it is thought, mine the Bible's apocalyptic writings for inside information about earth's final days, and then use it, like fugitives, to navigate a safe journey to the Advent, a flight through, and eventually out of, the world. Vulnerable to harm, feckless against the march of evil, end-time believers focus on assuring a getaway—on watching out for heretics and enemies, on avoiding deception and danger. When these true believers do connect with the people outside their own circle, the purpose is to communicate warnings and confide esoteric information; it is, in short, to facilitate escape through talk.[4]

But neither spirituality as escape nor mission as talk does justice to authentic biblical eschatology. Nor, I imagine, does either satisfy, let alone galvanize, thoughtful church members in Adventism's older strongholds. Persons who are deeply broken and discouraged may find mere escape seductive; they may also gain satisfaction from having inside information to divulge. But those who remain adventurous, who take delight in the creativity and accomplishment available to creatures made in the image of God, gravitate to grander dreams. They want to pursue good and subvert evil; to shape a better home, neighborhood, town or world; to plant a garden, start a business, run a clinic, mend a city — put a song, somehow, in human hearts.

In this way, adventurous people resemble the great protagonists of Scripture, for whom mere escape and mere information would have been sheer poverty of spirit. Neither escape nor mere information would, in their view, have seemed important enough or daring enough to rivet energy and inspire praise — or to count as the authentic calling of God. After all, from Abraham through the prophets to Jesus and the apostles, the spiritual life meant fellowship and collaboration with the Maker of all things, the One who gives us minds and hearts and calls us to adventure, blessing and joy. With such a God, and with such a calling, the grander the dream the better.

Our own story and agenda, our own shared life, bequeath us, I believe, a truly compelling spirituality and mission. Near the center of the Adventist experience, as we know and gladly affirm, is eschatology — the understanding of God's End for the world. If we are impoverished by the dominant eschatology, the deeper eschatology of Adventism can renew and enrich our life.

In what follows I will suggest that this deeper eschatology calls us into the fellowship of the Remnant for the purpose — the magnificent purpose—of peacemaking. Our story, agenda and shared life compel us to become, or to aspire to become, nothing less than—the Peacemaking Remnant. This aspiration constitutes the grander dream we need, and reflects both our own story as a people and the story of God as told in Scripture.

The Dominant Eschatology

A new example of the dominant, or as we might say, "official," Adventist eschatology is Norman Gulley's recent book, *Christ is Coming*. Gulley, who teaches at Southern Adventist University, reflects for nearly 600 pages on themes familiar to Adventists from sermons and seminars on "last-day events." Pre-publication praise for the book included assurance from the editor of the Adventist Review that it is "a major contribution to the Adventist Church and to Christian thought in general" and additional assurance, from a professor, that it represents "the present heartbeat of centrist Adventist eschatology." This and similar praise is printed at the book's beginning, alongside a foreword by the (former) General Conference President, who says the author's work is "crucial" for the church's "understanding and safety."[5]

In his way, Gulley does indeed provide seed and sustenance for the rejuvenation of the church. He upholds Christ and the ideal of a relationship with Christ. He understands history as a conflict between Christ and Satan, and sees the cross as a "decisive" victory in that conflict. He challenges the liberal devaluation of eschatology and suggests that survival-of-the-fittest naturalism brings in its train "degrading social results."

He is rightly suspicious, moreover, of empires and church-state alliances. As for plotting the schedule of last-day of events, long a preoccupation in our community, he forswears date-setting altogether and attempts only a "general view of the journey," not a detailed account.[6]

In all these respects, Gulley offers hints of the deeper eschatology of Adventism. Each point is important; none is more important than his upholding of Christ. Although he never dwells at length on the image of the church as remnant, he does remark that "only resting in [Christ] will carry the remnant through the final crisis."[7] In this he is surely right—the point would hold, I suppose, for any crisis—and because he says it he is surely to be thanked. Unfortunately, Christ does not sufficiently control the discourse in his book, and this fact accounts most of all for the impoverishment that marks this expression of the church's dominant of eschatology.

The Jesus of the Gospels took for granted that the earth is God's creation, recipient of divine care, open to human striving. He thought of himself as in the lineage of Abraham, Moses and the prophets, mediators all of earthly truth and blessing. He saw God's Kingdom—God's politics, as you might say—touching the here and now, and when he enjoined apocalyptic watchfulness, he said that truly faithful watchers stay at their appointed earthly business, attentive to the space around them as well as to the time.[8] Spirituality did not mean withdrawal and escape; it meant engagement and stewardship: disciples invest their resources to the end, according to Matthew 25, and at the Great Assize confront a single question: Have you taken care of people?[9]

If faithful watchers look to the "true ending of the world," and live in its light,[10] that true ending, after all, is Christ, the same Christ who in becoming flesh sanctified the earth and embraced the human prospect.[11] This is what Gulley's expression of the dominant eschatology mainly misses. He understands, truly, that the Second Advent delivers us from "extinction." He understands, truly, that human effort alone neither assures nor even hastens the final triumph of Christ.[12] But in his zeal to resist the kind of shallow, feel-good optimism that plays down the Second Advent, Gulley effectively denies the First Angel's presumption, expressed in Revelation 14, that despite sin and crisis God is still the maker of "heaven and earth." Gulley effectively denies, in other words, that the world is still God's good creation and still receptive to human creativity and care.[13]

12

When he makes Kingdom-building God's work alone, and in no sense ours; when he discredits all efforts "to change society"; when he scorns not only the myth of tidy upward progress but the whole idea of "human improvement"; when he renounces Christian involvement in "the political arena" and declares that the world can only get "worse,"[14] he simply departs from the biblical point of view. What is more, in lapsing into an eschatology of resignation, he contradicts his own declaration, much earlier in the book, that at the cross Christ made a "decisive difference" for a world which is "no longer Satan's world."[15]

When Christ Controls the Discourse

The difference the cross makes reminds us, again, that Christ is the key. If Christ controlled the discourse of eschatology, meager vision would give way to abundance. The spirit of Christ — and the spirit of the prophets and apostles — would call us into fellowship and collaboration with the Maker of Heaven and Earth, and in both the speaking and living out of eschatology we would aspire to be the Remnant God intends: not escape artists but peacemakers, "co-workers with Christ," as Ellen White said, in the work of redemption.[16]

From the start, Adventists have seen themselves as a faithful minority witnessing for God in the midst of last-day crisis; and from the start they have embraced the biblical motif of the Remnant as a way to idealize this vision.[17] When this motif is put to narcissistic use — as in the claim, "We are the Remnant Church," or "Only Adventists are God's true Remnant," — it makes thoughtful members cringe,[18] and should. But everyone can agree, I think, that we are called to be the Remnant. That is our heritage, and when it generates high aspiration, not self-important posturing, that heritage is both honorable and illuminating.

Consider now where it leads. Consider the spirituality and mission the Remnant ideal can bequeath to those who look past mere convention to the deeper eschatology of Scripture.

Both the dominant and deeper eschatologies uphold the Christ of the Gospels as, in Gulley's words, the "clearest, most authentic, revelation of God."[19] That being so, the Christ of the gospels must control how we interpret Scriptural testimony concerning the Remnant.

Begin, then, with Jesus' reference, in Luke 12:32, to his disciples as a "little flock." The reference belongs to the larger gospel theme of good (or indifferent) shepherds, as voiced, for example, in Matthew 9:36, where Jesus feels compassion for people who are "harassed and helpless, like sheep without a shepherd," and in Luke 15:3-7, where he tells the parable of the shepherd who finds and rejoices over a single lost sheep.[20] The larger theme reflects, in turn, the similar imagery of shepherds and sheep that is found in the Hebrew prophets. And in a key passage, Jeremiah 23:1-6, this imagery is tied explicitly to the remnant ideal. Against a setting of evil shepherds and scattered sheep, God declares, in verse 3: "'Then I myself will gather the remnant of my flock,'" and declares further, in verse 4, that this remnant will enjoy generous care: "'they shall not fear any longer, or be dismayed, nor shall any be missing.'" In chapter 31, where the theme is return from exile, Jeremiah again links the imagery of the remnant and the gathered flock, here envisioning that his nation's restoration involves the renewal of hearts and the forgiveness of sins.[21]

In Ezekiel 34 God again makes a promise to "scattered" sheep, to the victims of indifferent or evil leaders. According to verses 11-23, God will "'seek'" these victims out, and "'rescue'" and "'feed'" them, and "'bind up'" their injured and "'strengthen'" their weak and given them all a new leader, "'my servant David,'" who will be "'their shepherd.'" Verses 25 and following then say that God will "make with them a covenant of peace," and in this condition of peace, as these verses go on to say, freedom and safety prevail; justice overcomes oppression and plenty supplants poverty. A few chapters later, when Ezekiel's theme is return from exile, and he again evokes the imagery of the "shepherd" and refers to the "covenant of

14

peace," he envisions, as Jeremiah does, the cleansing and renewing of human hearts.[22]

So, although Jesus never in the Gospels uses the term "remnant," he borrows from the prophets the language of the remnant: the pictures of the scattered and the suffering gathered with their Maker into a fellowship of peace, a sweeping wholeness of life under the mercy and care of God. And when the Gospel writers interpret Jesus, they invoke shepherd prophecies and promises of peace that recall the remnant gathering foretold in Jeremiah: Jesus' birth in Bethlehem, Matthew says, fulfills the prophet Micah's vision of a ruler from that town who will "feed his flock" and be "the one of peace"; Jesus' coming, Luke says, echoing Isaiah, gives light to those in "'darkness'" and guides their feet into "'the way of peace.'"[23]

One result, then, of reading the remnant motif in the light of Christ is recovery of the sense that, first of all, the remnant is the recipient of divine favor. The motif becomes what it always was for Israel, an evocation of grace. In calling us to be the remnant, God calls us into wholeness of life under the divine care, into a compassionate and rejuvenating fellowship. A difference in the Gospel accounts is that this fellowship revolves around Jesus himself, even after, as both Matthew and John declare, his ascension into heaven.[24] Another is that here, unmistakably, the prophetic dream of a community that reaches foreigners and outcasts begins to be realized.[25] But the differences underscore the fact that the fellowship is compassionate and rejuvenating, an expression of God's transforming grace.

Jesus' reference to the disciples as "little flock," in Luke 12:32, occurs as Jesus, having "set his face resolutely toward Jerusalem,"[26] is making his journey to the city that was the center of his culture. Along the way and upon arrival, he explains and embodies his mission–his vision of God, his all-encompassing compassion, his critique of misleaders, his hope and his vigilance in the face of danger, his evocation of a politics of non-violence, his generosity even to those who hate and harm him.[27] And as he approaches Jerusalem on a donkey's foal,

15

recalling Zechariah's dream of the peaceable kingdom, jubilant disciples echo the song of peace sung to the shepherds at Jesus' birth.[28]

Disciples, indeed, echo the deeds as well as the words of the Kingdom. As the "little flock" accompany Jesus on the journey to Jerusalem, they undertake the same dangerous mission, and find in that mission the same joy and fulfillment.[29] And they again and again hear reminders of their call—to follow their leader and to bear the cross and to become great through service.[30] This is how they, in David's words, "pursue peace"; it is how they plant their feet on "'the way of peace,'" as the prophecy foretold; it is how true disciples keep the commandments of God and hold fast to the faith of Jesus.[31]

Judging by Jesus' own example, the way of peace holds sway even in the most hazardous of times. Whether he is affirming the presence of the Kingdom or announcing apocalyptic urgency—or facing danger himself[32]—Jesus sticks by the journey to Jerusalem and the mission that prompted it. As peace was the point to begin with, and his message when the mission was accomplished—"'Peace be with you,'" he tells the astonished disciples on resurrection day—so peace was the heart his witness at its most vivid and harrowing point, his provocative entrance into Jerusalem.[33]

If the peril of that moment could not deter Jesus from his peacemaking, neither should any peril deter his followers from peacemaking. Above all as the End approaches, those "who try to make their life secure" depart from the way of faithfulness. The "little flock" keep "dressed for action"; they stay "alert"; they remain "at work" to the end.[34]

All this follows from the uplifting of Christ as the "clearest, most authentic, revelation of God."[35] All this suggests the heightened relevance, especially for those called to be the Remnant, of the simple words from the Sermon on the Mount: "'Blessed are the peacemakers, for they will be called the children of God.'"[36]

Here, judging from the whole Gospel and from the prophets who anticipate the Gospel, lies as profound a clue as any to the mission of Remnant, those who, against the drift of the dominant culture, struggle to uphold the integrity of the people of God.[37] Here a call goes forth to all who know the divine favor and everlasting grace, a call to all who fear God, who scorn Babylon, who hold fast to the faith of Jesus.

It is a call to espouse a grander dream than resignation, to refuse withdrawal and escape and to embrace engagement and stewardship. It is a call to follow Jesus, to proclaim and embody the compassion of God, the politics of God, the peace of God, and thus to be, like the great protagonists of Scripture, mediators of the divine blessing.[38] It is a call, in short, to be a "prophetic minority," a minority "ready to think and act ahead of the community as a whole, and so keep alive the vision of God's redemptive way."[39]

All this belongs to the heartbeat of hope, authentic Christian hope. But in the dominant eschatology all of it is missing, and the consequence is not only loss in well-directed energy but also gain in misdirected energy—as epitomized in Adventist complicity with Nazi and Rwandan genocide, or with the Koresh fiasco in Waco, Texas.[40]

Adventism's Deeper Vision

Still, the deeper vision also comes through in Adventist life. It comes through in the example of persons like Ellen White and Fernando Stahl, John Weidner and Desmond Doss, Vladimir Shelkov and Milan Suslic.[41]

It comes through in the witness of Adventist leaders who, during the Spanish-American War, denounced their nation's military aggression; in the 1921 Autumn Council letter to Warren Harding asking, in the name of the "Prince of Peace," for "limitation of armaments" and "amelioration of human woe"; in the 1985 Annual Council statement summoning the faithful to advance "social, cultural, and economic justice" and to urge the nations to "beat their 'swords into plowshares.'"[42]

17

It comes through, too, in Adventist writing—in the eschatologies of John Brunt, Sakae Kubo, Charles Teel and Roy Branson, in the ecclesiologies of Steven G. Daily, Gottfried Oosterwal and Zdravko Plantak.[43] All these resources go unnoticed, or virtually unnoticed, in the dominant eschatology, but all illuminate, in a fresh and mobilizing way, the fundamental truth of the Adventist pioneers: that a faithful minority must bear witness to the victory of Christ in the midst of last-day crisis.

For the biblical Remnant, spirituality is not escape, it is fellowship; mission is not (mere) talk, it is peacemaking. Amid surrounding allusions to the remnant, the prophet Micah declares in his classic summary that the truly faithful "walk humbly" with God while doing "justice" and loving "kindness."[44]

This is true worship—true veneration, indeed, of the Sabbath—and this is the outlook and practice that give rise, in the end, to peace.[45] This is what it means to hold fast to the faith of Jesus and to be co-workers of the risen Christ in the work of redemption. This is why the church matters—and why evangelism matters. The church and its champions exist to widen the circle of those who, by faith in the Victory of God and by a conspiracy of peacemaking, subvert all that is evil and build up all that is good.

The Peacemaking Remnant enter confidently, then, into fellowship and collaboration with the Maker of Heaven and Earth. They know that in a world doomed to decline, Ellen White could not have founded a medical college, or Fernando Stahl taught Indians to read, or John Weidner saved Jews from the Holocaust; nor could Anabaptists have imagined religious liberty, or suffragists secured the vote for women, or unarmed dissenters brought the Berlin Wall to the ground.

The Peacemaking Remnant realize, of course, that prophetic transformation meets resistance and interruption. They know that despite the goodness of creation, God's people sing their songs in a strange land, face disappointment and dreams deferred, suffer bitter anguish.[46] They know that the advance of the Kingdom is neither placid nor predictable; it is turbulent and startling—a saga of setbacks and upheavals, of constant uneasiness with the present order, constant empathy with human brokenness, constant readiness to meet new challenges. But they press on, looking to the climax—the grand surprise—of the Second Coming, when God's peacemakers sing the song of the Lamb and hear thunderous words of victory from the heavenly throne.

All this, I submit, is hope in a biblical key. It is a hope grand enough and daring enough to rivet energy and inspire praise— today. And in the light of the dominant eschatology, it seems clear that this deeper vision of spirituality and mission will, if we embrace it, both change and steady our minds, both revise and confirm the way we live. It is at once a departure and a return.

On a journey into fellowship and peacemaking we will, as the poet said, "arrive where we started/and know the place for the first time."[47]

The Peacemaking Remnant: Seven Theses
by Charles Scriven

1. **Biblical peace, or** *shalom,* **is a sweeping wholeness of life.** Where *shalom* prevails, freedom and safety prevail; justice overcomes oppression; plenty supplants poverty; joy defeats gloom and shame. Peace *is* salvation; salvation *is* peace (Eze. 34:25-30; Isa. 52:7,8).

2. **The biblical remnant is made up of God's partners in peacemaking.** Against fashion and tyranny alike, they walk in God's way, beaming light into darkness, winning minds and hearts to the way of peace (Gen. 1:27; 12:2; Isa. 1:1 to 2:4, Isa. 42:1-4; 44:1; 46:3; Rev. 12:17; Matt. 5:11-16).

3. **Jesus defines the Christian vocation: he came to "fulfill" the law of life, to show its ultimate meaning and purpose.** Through the resurrection God validated Jesus' accomplishment, declaring that his words and deeds reveal the will—the very heart—of God (Matt. 5:17, 18; Rom. 1:1-4; Heb. 1:1-4).

4. **According to Jesus, God is generous to all, friends and enemies alike.** God refuses to manipulate outcomes by evil means. The love of God is nonviolent and unconditional—this is the divine perfection we are called to emulate (Matt. 5:38-48; Rom. 12:14-21; Heb. 1:1-4).

5. **Jesus announces and inaugurates a "Kingdom"—a new ideal, a new community, a new path to peace.** Heavenly in origin, this Kingdom is earthly in relevance: its attitudes and practices are a radical form of personal, social and political responsibility (Matt. 4:23; 5:1-16; 6:10; Luke 4:16-19).

6. **Christian peacemaking is the unswerving effort to overcome evil with good.** Based on confidence that generosity wins hearts away from evil, and that unearned suffering can be redemptive, it is the *practice* of the change we wish to see (Matt. 5:13-16; John 17:17-21; Rom. 12:21; Eph. 2:13,14; Rev. 5).

7. **In this light evangelism must be redefined.** Teaching Scripture and enlarging church membership is the (indispensable) shell of evangelistic mission. The heart of it, however, is peacemaking—the making of human wholeness through the practice and preaching of the love of God (Matt. 28:18-20, in light of the above).

20

"Would God that all the LORD's people were prophets, and that the LORD would put his spirit upon them!" (Num. 11:29b).
"The testimony of Jesus is the spirit of prophecy" (Rev. 19:10b).

2

A People of Prophecy
Recovering the Biblical Role of the Prophets

ZDRAVKO PLANTAK

Two hunters, in determined pursuit of wild buffalo, chartered a plane to fly them into forest territory. Both succeeded in their mission of bringing down a specimen of the prize game. When, two weeks later, the pilot came to take them back, he took a look at the animals they had shot and said, "This plane won't take more than one wild buffalo. You'll have to leave the other behind."

"But last year the pilot let us take two in a plane this size," the hunters protested. The pilot was doubtful, but finally said, "Well, if you did it last year I guess we can do it again."

So the plane took off with the three men and two buffaloes. But it couldn't gain height and crashed into a neighboring hill. The men climbed out and looked around. One hunter said to the other, "Where do you think we are?" The other inspected the surroundings and said, "I think we're about two miles south of where we crashed last year." A highly selective account of the past led to action producing disastrous results.

Seventh-day Adventists believe they are called to a prophetic role in the end time.[1] Without a clearer and fuller picture of biblical role of the prophets, however, we risk repeating the fate of the greedy and complacent hunters.

If we are to constitute a prophetic minority at the end of the world's history, our role should be comparable to the role of the prophets in Hebrew society. Seventh-day Adventist understanding of the role of prophets and prophecies has been primarily of a futuristic and apocalyptic nature. However, predicting the future was only a secondary role of the prophets of ancient Israel. Their primary role was that of social reformers and visionaries – visionaries of what can be and what should be.

The Hebrew term translated "prophet" – *nabhi* – comes from an Akkadian root which means "to call," "to announce." *Nabhi* is first used in connection with Abraham (Gen 20:7). However, it becomes a popular term with Moses (Deut 34:10). As provider of the moral law, Moses becomes a standard of comparison for all other prophets (Deut 18:15ff).

Enid Mellor points out that

> the biblical prophets wrote about the times in which they lived, and prediction was less important than warning and exhortations. They believed themselves to be commissioned and inspired by Yahweh to speak his word to their contemporaries – to point them away from their foolish ways and to show them true religion and morality.[2]

Mellor, like many modern students of prophetic literature, realizes that the Old Testament prophets had several important roles. They:

1) **were social, political and religious leaders who proclaimed the law;**
2) **guarded the spiritual life of the nation by being visionaries.** They dared to imagine how the life was supposed to be with what Walter Brueggemann, in his now-famous book title, calls the *Prophetic Imagination;*[3]
3) **mediated between the people and their God;**
4) **predicted future judgment but also hope that God would bring to the most disadvantaged members of society**.

In sum, they were interested in international affairs and the future while in the same breath they counseled and influenced social structures of their own generation in their own locality.

They could be therefore described as theological and social reformers and visionaries.

Essential Elements of Prophetic Teaching

Four essential elements[4] emerge from prophetic teachings. First, the warnings which prophets bring are always a **matter of life and death**. Every warning, if not taken seriously, is followed by long-lasting consequences. We see, for example, in Isaiah 40-55 how serious consequences awaited Israel – the captivity and exile. The prophets called Israel to reject evil and death and choose God, moral behavior and, consequently, life.[5] This principle is nowhere better illustrated than in Deuteronomy 30:15-20:

> See, I have set before you today life and prosperity, death and adversity. If you obey the commandments of the LORD your God that I am commanding you today, by loving the LORD your God, walking in his ways, and observing his commandments, decrees, and ordinances, then you shall live and become numerous, and the LORD your God will bless you in the land that you are entering to possess. But if your heart turns away and you do not hear, but are led astray to bow down to other gods and serve them, I declare to you today you shall perish; you shall not live long in the land that you are crossing the Jordan to enter and possess. I will call heaven and earth to witness against you today that I have set before you life and death, blessings and curses. Choose life so that you and your descendants may live, loving the LORD your God, obeying him, and holding fast to him; for that means life to you and length of days, so that you may live in the land that the LORD swore to give to your ancestors, to Abraham, to Isaac, and to Jacob (Deut. 30:15-20).

The second element in prophetic teaching deals with **God's care for those who are without proper protection within the existing social structures (e.g. slaves, widows, orphans, debtors, the homeless, and strangers)**.

The biblical law requires (Ex 23:3 & Deut 16:19-20) that there should be no unjust differences between people. But in real life this ideal became perverted. As Brueggemann puts it, "... then [in ancient Israel] and now, eating that well means food is being taken off the table of another....Covenanting which takes brothers and sisters seriously had been replaced by consuming which regards brothers and sisters as products to be used."[5] The economics of equality had changed to the economics of affluence.

The prophetic alternative, what Brueggeman calls, "the primary prophetic agenda," offers the "possibility of passion...as the capacity and readiness to care, to suffer, to die, and to feel" for other people. Ultimately, God "is one whose person is presented as passion and pathos, the power to care, the capacity to weep, the energy to grieve and to rejoice." And prophets must think with God, "not whether it is realistic or practical or viable but whether it is imaginable...[And therefore] think an alternative thought."[6]

David Noel Freedman observes that

the characteristic way of a prophet in Israel is that of poetry and lyric. The prophet engages in future fantasy. The prophet does not ask if the vision can be implemented, for questions of implementation are of no consequence until the vision can be imagined. The imagination must come before the implementation.[7]

Furthermore, God promises to be a support and help to those who do not have anybody: he hears their cries, sees their suffering, and brings help when his human agents fail to do so. The prophets talk about the alienation of those who grab land and "add house to house and join field to field" until they become alone in the land (see Isa 5:8). This process of materialism, mirrored in our own time and expressed in the accumulation of material goods beyond the point of realistic needs, ends in isolation and in the loss of any meaningful human existence and relationship among people.

Thirdly, **God seeks obedience and justice rather than a formal worship or sacrifice.** The sacrificial system and religious festivals (including the observance of Sabbath) were important. But ethical behavior springing from right motives was even more important ("doing the truth" instead of only "having the truth"). And the basic motive was to be love which responds to God's love, God's choice and God's calling (Deut 7:6-11). Therefore, the motive for ethical behavior and social action is an answer to God's love, which he expressed in covenants with human beings (1 John 4:9-10).

Just look at Isaiah 58, a chapter that our Adventist pioneers quoted over and over again:

"Why do we fast but you do not see?
"Why humble ourselves, but you do not notice?"
Look, you serve your own interest on your fast day, and oppress all your workers.

Look, you fast only to quarrel and to fight and to strike with a wicked fist. Such fasting as you do today will not make your voice heard on high....

Is not this the fast that I choose: to loose the bonds of injustice, to undo the thongs of the yoke, to let the oppressed go free, and to break every yoke?

Is it not to share your bread with the hungry, and bring the homeless poor into your house; when you see the naked to cover them, and not to hide yourself from your own kin?

Then your light shall break forth like the dawn, and your healing shall spring up quickly; your vindicator shall go before you, and the glory of the Lord shall be your rear guard (Isa. 58:3-4, 6-8)

A cobbler once sought the counsel of Rabbi Isaac of Ger, asking: "Tell me what to do about my morning prayer. My customers are poor men who have only one pair of shoes. I pick up their shoes late in the evening and work on them most of the night; at dawn there is still work to be done if the men are to have their shoes ready before they go to work. Now my question is: What should I do about my morning prayer?"

"What have you been doing till now?" the Rabbi asked.

"Sometimes I rush through the prayer quickly and get back to my work – but then I feel bad about it. At other times I let the hour of prayer go by. Then too I feel a sense of loss and can almost hear my heart sigh, 'What an unlucky man I am, that I am not able to make my morning prayer.'"

The Rabbi responded, "If I were God I would value that sigh more than the prayer."

The fourth element of the prophetic role is of **eschatological-apocalyptic character**. In this element of prophetic teaching, the prophet goes outside his immediate domain and speaks about the global picture of human history. And, ultimately, the prophet speaks about <u>hope</u> that is so often non-existent among people who live their lives in hopeless day-to-day survival situations and modes. At its center, prophetic eschatology is an affirmation that **God will** *succeed* in his desire for his creation, that he shall win the battle between good and evil and inevitably bring salvation to his people both in the spiritual sense but also in the physical liberation from bondage of hopelessness, poverty and this earth's disadvantage.

"It is the vocation of the prophet to keep alive the ministry of imagination, to keep on conjuring and proposing alternative futures to the single one that the establishment of the day wants to urge as the only thinkable one," writes Jack Provonsha.[8]

Seventh-day Adventists have usually emphasized the fourth aspect of the prophetic role, especially in its evangelistic and theological sense. Too often, though, rather then portraying a theology of hope, we have turned the prophet eschatological message into one of doom and gloom which is more concerned with scaring and frightening people than the good news that God is in control and will finally conquer evil and establish the good rule of his heavenly government.

The Seventh-day Adventist identity as a "prophetic movement" has usually been conceived of as "a movement preoccupied with making predictions" as well as "a movement with a special interest in studying and interpreting predictive prophecy." But, as Provonsha says, Adventism as a prophetic movement should be defined more in terms of function and role; in other words we should think of ourselves as a people with a mission to the world.[9] Therefore, to be faithful to our prophetic calling we must take seriously all aspects of ministry of the biblical prophets, incorporating the primary, or social, role of prophets.

Examples of the Primary (Social) Role of Prophets

The prophets of the Old Testament did not invent new social, economic or moral responsibilities. They affirmed that the ideal for Hebrew society as a whole, and its people as individuals, was set in the legislation of the *covenant* between God and Israel. They regarded justice, as a basis of the law and the pillar of society, as binding for all ages. The guidance they gave to Israel regarding social, ethical and economic relationships were clearly based on the Mosaic Law as expressed in the Ten Commandments.

The moral law, as an expression of the character of God and as God's desire for human fulfillment, was always high on the agenda of Adventist theology. For us the Decalogue is still valid as a great moral guideline binding upon all people who desire to live in perfect harmony with God and with other human beings in every age. It is not, and has never been, the means of salvation (Rom 4:1-3; Heb 11). However the fruitage of salvation is obedience to these precepts that God himself gave to humanity (Ex 31:18).

For a complete understanding of what God means by his moral law, a Christian must turn to the God incarnate. Jesus, in his most remarkable sermon about the law (some call the Sermon on the Mount the second Sinai)[10] claimed that he did not come to abolish the law but to fulfill it (Matt 5:17). He continued:

> "Anyone who breaks one of the least of these commandments and teaches others to do the same will be called least in the   kingdom of heaven, but whoever practices and teaches these commands will be called great in the kingdom of heaven" (Matt 5:19).

When challenged to give an account of what he thought was the most important commandment, Jesus did not allow himself to be drawn into making the mistake of selecting one and over-emphasizing it. Rather, he summed up the law and the prophets into a remarkably concise but powerful phrase borrowed from Deuteronomy 6: "'Love the LORD your God with all your heart and with all your soul and with all your mind.' This is the first and the greatest commandment. And the second is like it: 'Love your neighbor as yourself'" (Matt 22:37-39; cf. Deut 6:4-5). Asked at another occasion, Who is my neighbor?, Jesus answered eloquently in a parable that our neighbor is everyone who is in need, regardless of race, nationality or caste (Luke 10:29-37).

The universality of the Old Testament account of the moral law (Ex 20:1-17 and Deut 5:1-22) and Jesus' elaboration of it (Matthew 5-7) require respect for and guarding of human rights. If God is interested in relationships between human beings, and he demonstrated the desire to regulate these relationships with the last six commandments of the Decalogue and with the numerous sayings of Jesus, his children should uplift these regulations and apply them to every situation in life.

A commandments-keeping people, as Seventh-day Adventists desire to be, should be the first to foster good relations with their neighbors. Whenever there is a violation of the love-principle in the world they ought to be among the first to condemn it and to seek ways to eliminate injustice, inequality, bad relationships, and violation of human rights in general in order to be true to their calling of the people of the law.

But at times we have made out of these wonderful instructions of God, limitations and burdens that have often oppressed rather then liberated people. How contrary to the divine intention!

An intrigued congregation speculated as to why their rabbi disappeared each week on the eve of the Sabbath. They suspected he was secretly meeting the Almighty, so they deputized one of their members to follow him.

This is what the man saw: the rabbi disguised himself in peasant clothes and served a paralyzed Gentile woman in her cottage, cleaning out the room and preparing a Sabbath meal for her. When the spy got back, the congregation asked: "Where did the rabbi go? Did he ascend to heaven?"

"No," the man replied, "he went even higher!"

This is exactly where a tablets-of-stone-religion becomes a new-heart-religion, as God intended it in the first place. The poet Kabir says: "What good is it if the scholar pores over words and points of this and that but his chest is not soaked dark with love? What good is it if the ascetic clothes himself in saffron robes, but is colorless inside? What good is it if you scrub your ethical behavior till it shines, but there is no music inside?"

We find in Amos, Hosea and Isaiah powerful examples of the passion for social justice expressed by all the prophets. Amos pointed to the following sins of the nation: exploitation and oppression of the poor (4:1; 5:11; 8:4-6); corrupt and degenerate religious practice (2:4,6); corruption of justice and righteousness (5:7-10; 6:12); unnecessary riches (6:4); and neglect of God's law (2:8; 8:5). He saw a solution to these sins in repentance (4:12.13; 5:4-13) or, if sins were not repented, eventually in punishment and judgment (2:5, 13-16; 3:2; 5:25-27).

Hosea termed prostitution (4:11-18), lying (4:2; 7:1), violence and murder (4:2; 6:8-9), robbery (7:1; 4:2), drunkenness (4:11; 7:5), idolatry (4:12; 8:4; 13:2), and rebellion against God (9:15; 13:16) as the greatest sins of his time. His proposed solution was again repentance or destruction in God's judgment (5:1-14; 8:1-9; 14:1).

Isaiah marked the sins of God's people of his time as idolatry (2:8), injustice (5:7; 59:8), bloodshed (59:7), rebellion (1:5; 57:4), neglect of widows (1:23; 10:2), heavy drinking (5:11; 28:1-7) and oppression of the poor (3:14-15; 10:2). He was a citizen of a vibrant city—Jerusalem in the eighth century B.C. He was consulted by kings on the great issues of the day. He did not shy away from political involvement, or from getting involved with issues of justice and socio-economic evils of his day. He made his views on such matters known even when he was not consulted. Issues of state and national security greatly concerned him. He was active, charismatic and very passionate.

29

In Joseph Robinson's words, "For [Isaiah] the integrity, more, the very existence of his faith, was dependent upon the decisions taken on political issues."[11]

Just by scanning through Isaiah 1 and 2 (see especially 1:11, 13-17, 21-23; 2:3-4,7, 10-19) we can see the strength of prophetic conviction. Isaiah is not timid; he speaks with full prophetic conviction and imagination.

Isaiah's message tells of God's punishment of Israel, particularly the kingdom of Judah, and of the punishment of the nations, for idolatry and injustice; and of God's subsequent redemption of the people of Israel. Both the punishment and redemption begin in Jerusalem/Zion, reaching from there to encompass the nations of the world. Although the message is universal in scope, it is never separated from its historic center – the people of Israel.

Brueggemann rightly identifies several modern themes to which Isaiah's ancient message speaks: consumerism, conspicuous consumption, the "wanton exhibitionism of the wealthy," "shameless luxury," exploitation of the vulnerable and resourceless, covetous agribusiness of "avaricious landowners," self indulgence, injustice, urban decline, hypocrisy, militarism, social exploitation, geopolitics of superpowers, and nuclear waste.[12]

The Role of the New Testaments Prophets

The role of the prophets in the New Testament was not very different from that in the Old Testament. John the Baptist, whom Jesus called the greatest prophet of all time (Matt 11:9-11), invited the people of Israel to repent and to produce good fruit (Matt 3:2-10). After querying whether Jesus was the Messiah, he received a message from Jesus which he could understand, appreciate, and identify with. Jesus said: "Go back and report to John what you hear and see: The blind receive sight, the lame walk, those who have leprosy are cured, the deaf hear, the dead are raised, and the good news is preached to the poor" (Luke 7:22b). This was a powerful testimony to the true prophet's concerns.

Just imagine if we were representing Jesus our Lord to people here on earth, and they came and asked, "Is Seventh-day Adventism a true representative of Christ?" "Are they true prophets?" Would people be able to respond about our mission in terms that Jesus responded describing his work? Would people say about us, "here are the people that have major satellite evangelistic campaigns," or "the blind receive sight, the lame walk, those who have leprosy are cured, the deaf hear, the dead are raised, and the good news is preached to the poor?"

Jesus of Nazareth was greatly concerned with the social and economic justice of his time. In his inaugural speech he came to proclaim freedom to the captives, to release the oppressed and to proclaim the acceptable year of the Lord. (Luke 4:18-21)[13] Jesus not only preached about issues of social concern, he also practiced his social beliefs. He demonstrated through his ministry that nobody was outside of his interest. And he demanded nothing less from his followers. Even in the most famous of his eschatological discourses, when his closest followers asked him about his *parousia* and "the end of the age," Jesus not only answered in terms of the outside events but also in terms of what his followers must do (Matt 24:1-25:46).

Parallel to proclaiming the gospel, the task of the church was to feed the hungry, give drink to the thirsty, be hospitable to the stranger, clothe the poor, visit the prisoner, and look after the sick. The social concern thus expressed was to be one of the primary tasks of the community awaiting the final realization of the kingdom of Jesus on earth.

For the contemporary Christian, writes John Brunt, the "eschatological vision of our future hope actually contributes to the content or shape of our daily lives. It helps us see how we should live responsibly here and now."[14] How we treat others in this world will not bring about the kingdom of God, but it should prove that this kingdom is in our hearts, that we are the new creatures who entered the sphere of the kingdom of grace

31

and that we anticipate the fulfillment of promises of the kingdom of glory in the near future.

The Prophetic Community Today

To fulfill the vocation of a "prophetic movement", Seventh-day Adventists must balance the proclamations about future events with calling people back to God-given principles of socio-economic justice, Christian ethics and human rights based on the moral law of the Old Testament and the explanation of it by the greatest of all Jewish prophets, and founder of the Christian church—Jesus Christ. Not only that we should proclaim these principles but we should embody them.

Numbers 11 relates what commentator Ellen Davis calls a "tangled tale of manna and quails, greed and prophecy."[15] Her analysis draws together in a powerful way the significance of the biblical prophets for today.

The people of Israel have just left Sinai in their sojourn through the desert. They received nourishment from the reliable provision of "manna" from God. However, for some – the "riffraff" (11:4) – a steady bread-of-heaven-only diet gets old pretty quickly. They crave meat, and demand that God serve it to them.

Intriguingly, they get a double answer. First, the angry answer, which Davis paraphrases as: "You want meat? I'll give you meat; you'll eat meat till it comes out your nose!" (11:20) – and God pours on the quails.

The second answer, which seems far less predictable though more benevolent, brings super-abundance in quite different form. God pours out a "spirit of prophecy" with such extravagance that it is not limited to those holding official credentials (11:24-26).

In a strange way, the story juxtaposes the seemingly incongruent: "unbridled greed" and "free-flowing prophecy." The Israelites' greed quite literally brought them to their graves. They died with the meat they had craved still in their mouths, and the mass burial site was called "Graves of Craving" (11:33-34). The Psalmist diagnosed the destructive power at work:

> because they had no faith in God,
> and did not trust his saving power
> [though] he had opened the doors of heaven.
> He had rained upon them manna to eat;
> The grain of heaven he had given them.
> Mortals ate bread of angels,
> He sent the food ENOUGH (Ps 78:22-25, emphasis supplied).

Their greed was symptomatic of a "spiritual malnutrition." With the manna, they had enough to eat. But because they did not trust in God, nothing – not even the "bread of angels" – would ever be enough.

Today, our insatiable craving for more than enough drives an ever-widening gap between the "haves" and the "have-nots," with many of the latter feeling that their only options are to die or fight back with whatever means they can find. Moreover, the planet itself is imperiled. Never in history have people lived so much beyond the level of subsistence as we do today, and the earth cannot indefinitely sustain the burden imposed by our "accustomed lifestyle." If we take scripture seriously, then we must believe that our greed, like Israel's, puts us in danger of God's devastating judgment.

This story in Numbers 11 is deeply disturbing, yet God's second extravagant answer to Israel's greed conveys an element of hope. A spirit of prophecy fills the seventy officially appointed elders. And then it overflows out into the camp of ordinary Israelites, so that Eldad and Medad start speaking God's truth. Joshua, fearing a threat to Israel's great God-anointed prophet and leader, complains that things are getting out of hand; it must stop at once.

"But Moses said to him, 'Are you jealous for my sake? Would that all the LORD'S people were prophets, and that the LORD would put his spirit on them' " (11:29).

Here at the Graves of Craving, I imagine prophets were trying to reorient the people from craving for meat to gratitude for manna, and to a greater awareness and concern for the poor and disadvantaged that we so easily forget in our craving and greed.

Davis summarizes eloquently:

> Another [important] function of the biblical prophets is to speak on behalf of the poor: those people, generally invisible to us, who suffer because of our selfishness. If we read the daily news in the light of their prophecy, we will recognize with increasing clarity that our lifestyle extracts a price from people most of us will never see in person, at least this side of the Resurrection. Third World countries have little to sell on the global market but the bones of their land – its minerals and forests – and the cheap labor of their people. They are exchanging short-term gain for ever deepening long-term poverty as their land is stripped and their water and air are polluted, in no small part by First World industries.[16]

There may be Joshuas today who will complain, "Stop them, make them be quiet. We should not be involved in that kind of prophetic task. The Lord will come and take care of this problem. Stop them!"

But the original *nabhi* – the model for all other prophets, responds: "Joshua, do you really think there isn't enough space for me *and* for Eldad and Medad? If only all God's people were prophets!"

God give us more prophets in Adventism, with more of the moral prophetic imagination that dares to speak out for the poor.

"And remember that thou wast a servant in the land of Egypt, and that the LORD thy God brought thee out thence through a mighty hand and by a stretched out arm: therefore the LORD thy God commanded thee to keep the sabbath day" (Deut. 5:15).
"Here are they that keep the commandments of God, and the faith of Jesus" (Revelation 14:12b).

3
Liberation Theology
The Genuine Article

CHARLES E. BRADFORD

"Princes shall come out of Egypt; Ethiopia shall soon stretch out her hands unto God" (Psalm 68:31)

The great prophecy of Psalm 68 has been a beacon of hope for the people of the African *diaspora*. It joins the purposes and plans of Yahweh with the Sabbath, the great sign and symbol of his power to create and redeem—the sign of liberation. Its reference to the exodus fired the imagination the early African-American church, lifting the spirits and giving hope to preachers and laypeople alike. They began to preach about the place of Ethiopia in the plans and purposes of God, looking upon the church of Abyssinia (Ethiopia) as the hidden church in wilderness through which God had maintained for Himself a witness down through the centuries.

The Sabbath in Ethiopia's Freedom Struggle

Throughout Ethiopia's history, fidelity to the ancient biblical Sabbath has been a defining feature of its national identity. The Sabbath was integral to Ethiopia's long, bitter, costly struggle to maintain her freedom from the European ecclesiastical establishment. The Ethiopians looked upon the Sabbath as a sign of their allegiance to God. It was covenantal; it stood for independence and self-determination.

"The history of the churches of Ethiopia and Abyssinia is especially significant," Ellen White comments in *The Great Controversy*.

> Amid the gloom of the Dark Ages, the Christians of Central Africa were lost sight of and forgotten by the world, and for many centuries they enjoyed freedom in the exercise of their faith. But at last Rome learned of their existence, and the emperor of Abyssinia was soon beguiled into an acknowledgment of the pope as the vicar of Christ. Other concessions followed. An edict was issued forbidding the observance of the Sabbath under the severest penalties [see Michael Geddes, *Church History of Ethiopia*, pp. 311, 312].
>
> But papal tyranny soon became a yoke so galling that the Abyssinians determined to break it from their necks. After a terrible struggle, the Romanists were banished from their dominions and the ancient faith was restored. . . .
>
> . . . [N]o sooner had they [the Ethiopians] regained their independence than they returned to obedience to the fourth commandment.[1]

Among Africans, *Ethiopianism* would become a code word for independence, freedom from foreign domination or rule in the political realm, and also for self-determination in matters of religion. For the Ethiopians, honoring the Sabbath meant recognition a higher power, a more superior court than those of the European imperialists and of their own rulers when these compromised the biblical faith. Though nameless and inexpressible, this conviction, this deep feeling, toppled thrones and brought emperors to their knees.

Symbol of Radical Liberation

In recent decades, theologians and biblical scholars in the so-called developing countries have taken up the theme of liberation. Having looked at the account of God's great deliverance in the Exodus, they are tremendously impressed with the power that He displayed in bringing His people out of bondage. African-American theologians and theologians from developing countries consider it their duty to focus on liberation. This is understandable. They are closer to those parts of the world in which the misery index is highest.

Traditional theology, they say, is done in ivory towers by those who are identified with the "haves." "God is on the side of the poor," they say, as they send out a ringing call for justice and equity. They challenge the industrialized nations and the Western religious establishment to identify with the poor and "get on God's side." Radical liberation theologians proclaim "Liberation whatever it takes, by whatever means," even revolutionary violence.

But radical liberation theology of this type is not really radical enough. The word "radical" means to get at the root of the matter. Political revolutions throw out one group of flawed creatures only to be succeeded by another.

Messiah Jesus came preaching an authentic theology of liberation:

> The Spirit of the Sovereign LORD is on me, because the Lord has anointed me to preach good news to the poor. He has sent me to bind up the brokenhearted, to proclaim freedom for the captives and release for the prisoners, to proclaim the year of the Lord's favor and the day of vengeance of our God, to comfort all who mourn (Isa. 61:1,2).

The message of Jesus, both radical and revolutionary, promised freedom to the nations—total freedom. He makes the Sabbath the sign of this liberation and independence.

The Ten Commandments, as found in Deuteronomy 5, are among the great proclamations about justice and human dignity, and the fourth commandment is its centerpiece. In this passage, Yahweh reveals himself as God of all flesh, the God of complete justice and equity. It is called the Sabbath Decalogue, and the Sabbath and justice are forever inseparable. The essence of Sabbath is social, always relational, always covenantal.

Indeed, the rendering of the Sabbath in Deuteronomy 5 speaks to the issues of fairness and justice that are relevant to any society, timeless. Harold MacMillan, Britain's prime minister, is reported to have called it "the first great worker protection act in history."[2]

The Sabbath commandment says in a very practical way, "Here is how it all must work out in real life and real time." It deals in specificities. It provides a concrete illustration of Micah's definitive statement: "He hath showed thee, O man, what is good, and what doth the LORD require of thee, but to do justly, and love mercy, and to walk humbly with thy God" (Micah 6:8).

> Keep the Sabbath day to sanctify it, as the LORD thy God hath commanded thee. Six days thou shalt labour, and do all thy work: But the seventh day is the Sabbath of the LORD the God: in it thou shalt not do any work, thou, nor thy son, nor thy daughter, nor thy manservant, nor thy maidservant, nor thine ox, nor thine ass, nor any of thy cattle, nor thy stranger that is within thy gates; that thy manservant and thy maidservant may rest as well as thou. And remember thou wast a servant in the land of Egypt, and that the LORD thy God brought thee out thence through a mighty hand and by a stretched out arm: there for the LORD thy God commanded thee to keep the sabbath day" (Deut. 5:12-15)

Christopher J.H. Wright observes that

> alongside this, there is the law commanding the just and prompt payment of wages to the most vulnerable workers (in Israel's case, the day labourers [24:14f])....In the Old Testament rejection of the sabbath principle was associated with exploitation and profiteering: Isaiah 1:13; Amos 8:4-6.
>
> The observance of the Sabbath is to be physical, concrete evidence of God' claim on us....It makes the primary relationship in our lives concrete and periodic.[3]

Sabbath is Yahweh's gift to humankind to keep them reminded of their creature status, to save them from the devastating effects of hubris on account of their achievements and accomplishments. These great prophetic words are the antidote for racism and oppression.

Old Testament scholar Bruce Birch writes,

> Thus Sabbath rest is to be available to all regardless of wealth or class, available to animals as well as humans (Ex. 20:10), reminding us of our common participation and worth as part of God's creation. Since we live in a world of inequalities, Sabbath then becomes a reminder that this is not as God intended it.[4]

Africa Suddenly Stretches Out Its Hand to God

The explosive growth of Christianity in Africa during twentieth century — unforeseen by expert observers — has been called the greatest miracle of modern missions. It made for a radical shift, a sea change, "a complete change in the center of gravity of Christianity" in the words of Andrew Walls.[5]

The people of sub-Saharan Africa, who for many centuries seemed unmoved by the claims of Messiah Jesus, suddenly have become ardent seekers, reaching out, stretching their hands toward Christianity, an outworking of that master prophecy of Psalm 68:31: "Ethiopia shall soon stretch out her hands unto God." The African continent has become the very center of the Christian New World.

This dramatic development was powered by independent movements with prophetic leaders inspired by the Ethiopian heritage of a Christianity that is truly African and free from European dominance. These independent churches broke away from the foreign domination of the African church, and the great prophets such as William Wadé Harris and Simon Kimbangu ventured to take up the mantle of the Old Testament prophets with little reference to, or consultation with, the established religious authorities, who were powerless to stop them.

39

Though quite diverse, the main prophetic movements and churches share a number of characteristics, which, placed together, create a new, rather African form of Christianity. Along with the prominence of healing, visions and dreams, a holy city, and certain kinds of rituals, many of the "modern African prophetic churches keep the Sabbath holy and adopt dietary and other prohibitions similar to those laid down in Leviticus, as the Ethiopians do," according to Elizabeth Isichei in *A History of Christianity in Africa*.[6]

The Key For an Oppressed People

One of the greatest of these prophets was Isaiah Shembe (c. 1870-1935), the most influential Zulu leader of his day. Filled with a burning desire to restore the former glory and dignity of the Zulu people, Shembe chose to do so through religion rather than the political process. He saw himself as an agent, under God, for the accomplishment of these goals and sought to mobilize the masses to make it a reality.

Shembe's deepest self-understanding was that of a chief/king, a people's king, the ideal Old Testament ruler. Through diligent study of the Bible, he established a moral basis for his message and his actions. In this he was reminiscent of the Old Testament prophets, always lashing out against the sins of commoners and leaders, religious and political.

Even though Shembe was thoroughly apolitical and urged his people to obey the established political authority, the government suspected him of preaching insurrection. Under almost all colonial administrations, the authorities were suspicious of any leader who had power with the people. Shembe's ultimate objective, his kingdom vision, was nothing less than the total revitalization of the Zulu people and, indeed, the whole of African society, but through peaceful and spiritual means.

He founded the Church of the Nazarites in 1911, convinced that the European forms of Christianity had failed to obey God's law as laid down in the Hebrew Bible. In particular he emphasized that only through observation of the Sabbath could the Zulu nation be fully restored to its independence and former glory.[7] In 1913, the year of the infamous South African land act making it illegal to sell property to Black Africans in restricted areas, a vision Shembe experienced at the mountain in southern Natal that became known as Nhlangkazi—"holy mountain" or Sinai—led him to declare that his church

accepted the Sabbath as God's holy day instead of the Christian Sunday. As a result of this vision, he considered the Sabbath to be the key to Zulu fortunes because it was the test of true obedience to God.[8]

Shembe's reasons for accepting the Sabbath are several. First, it is biblical. He arrived at this understanding from his study of the Bible. Second, he came to see the Sabbath as being important to the cause of liberation and freedom. Third, in Shembe's theology, the Sabbath is relevant to the wholeness and well-being of Africans and Africans in diaspora today. He provides us with a radical option. The Sabbath would be an affirmation of human worth, especially to the peoples of Africa and of African descent.

Two of Shembe's followers gave an eyewitness account of an experience on the mountain Nhlangakazi in 1922, in which Shembe proclaimed that

"the great ancient kingdoms abolished the day of the Lord....Because of its restrictions, the ancient kingdoms tried to push it aside and chose the day, which they liked, the Sunday, and they said, that they praised the resurrection of the Lord on that day."[9]

Shembe here pointed out the natural antipathy on the part of the ancient kingdoms toward the Sabbath. The Sabbath has its restrictions; it is a binding covenant that the King enjoins upon His subjects. It is to be expected that earthly rulers should resist the rule of Yahweh. They view it as a threat to and a dilution of their authority, and would rather have the people say, "We have no king but Caesar."

41

The tendency of all human rulers is toward absolute power and authority, which is Yahweh's prerogative. They find the covenant aspect of the Sabbath too restrictive, too binding. Furthermore, it interferes with commerce as well as with carnal pleasure (see Isa. 58).

Shembe recognizes that Sunday is always an import to Africa, brought to its shores by the Europeans. In this he is identifying those "great ancient kingdoms" that "abolished the day of the Lord." Clearly, these powers are the imperial church and her successors, who imposed the imposter day upon their subjects.

The Zulu prophet told his people that the Sabbath was a "great blessing" to those who observed it, but also warned that its restoration would bring conflict: "For when this day will become too difficult to keep for you, what will you do?...It may destroy all of you together with your coming generations." There would be difficulty associated with this day, hardship, persecution.

If I understand the testimony of the biblical witnesses correctly, controversy over this day has much to do with the final showdown between those cosmic forces to whom the people of the earth give their supreme allegiance, Messiah Jesus or the enemy of all righteousness.

The Final Freedom Struggle

For the Akan people of West Africa, one of the appellations for the High God is the great Nana. This is the name used to describe Yahweh as the universal Father. The great Nana is displeased by man's inhumanity to man. He is displeased whenever the social contract is broken. Joseph Danquah writes,

> Until man at last discovers the Nana of ultimate being, and not merely a small family or race or tribe or ethnic group, or larger unit of humanity such as Western or Asiatic, he stands under the judgment of God.[10]

This Akan understanding of the judgment and justice of God corresponds to Paul's great statement of belief: "Because he hath appointed a day, in the which he will judge the world in righteousness" (Acts 17:31).

Yahweh sees this failure to recognize Him as the supreme Nana as an attempt to place Him in a box, to manipulate Him, to use Him, to reduce Him to the status of a tribal god, and to deny Him His position as Father of all human beings—in African terms, to conjure Him.

There is a social contract that Yahweh imposed upon the human family at Creation (see 2 John 5). The Sabbath is a sign of the relationship existing between God and His people, a sign that they are His obedient subjects, that they keep holy His law. The observance of the Sabbath is the means ordained by God of preserving a knowledge of Himself and of distinguishing between His loyal subjects and the transgressors of His law.

When the "ancient nations" (the European ecclesiastical establishment) deliberately changed the day of worship from Saturday to Sunday, Yahweh was aggrieved because human beings had acted unilaterally and presumptuously. A dissonant note was brought in that fractured the harmony and peace that Yahweh wished for His children to enjoy.

In tampering with the contract—the law of Sinai, and especially the fourth commandment of that law, the Latin Church has defied Yahweh. They have removed that commandment from the law—the fourth—which makes all human beings equal.

It is good that the great Nana rises up in judgment: "At the set time that I appoint I will judge with equity" (Psalm 75:2, NRSV). His Fatherhood, His Nanahood, has been challenged: "Arise, O God, plead thine own cause; remember how the foolish man reproacheth thee daily" (Psalm 74:22).

The judge is the most awesome figure in the Old Testament. He combines in his person the executive, judicial, and legislative functions. In the Old Testament there is also the ideal king, who is the real moral force in the nation, the righteous defender and champion of the poor and powerless.

In the African culture, the chief was required to reflect the virtues of the great Nana. He was expected to embody all the characteristics of nobility and justice that are seen in the great Nana.

The chief must maintain the peace and harmony of the community. He must not allow any of his subjects to mar the good name or reputation of the kingdom. It is his duty to cleanse the camp of evil. The people expect no less. The Hebrew prophets call on Yahweh to rise up and execute judgment.

In the book of Revelation, the prophet John sees Yahweh fulfilling this role. He judges the universal community of nations and removes evil from their midst. His rising up results in a good community in which justice and equity prevail. The great Nana cannot leave the cosmos in disorder. He must restore *shalom*, that is, right relations and just conditions.

In order to accomplish His ultimate purpose for this planet, Yahweh will effect a greater deliverance than He did in Egypt. This time the whole world and all its people are involved.

The climax of the liberation struggle is described in sublime word pictures that speak across all of the divides that separate the family of man, barriers of race, social class, ethnicity, and gender: "After this I beheld, and lo, a great multitude, which no man could number, of all nations, and kindreds, and people, and tongues, stood before the throne, and before the Lamb, clothed with white robes, and palms in their hands" (Rev. 7:9).

One of the African proverbs says: "Hope is the pillar of the world." According to the biblical prophets, that hope is grounded in Yahweh's future: "For I know the plans I have for you, says the LORD, plans for welfare and not for evil, to give you a future and a hope" (Jer. 29:11, RSV).

> "And they overcame him by the blood of the Lamb, and by the
> word of their testimony; and they loved not their lives unto the
> death" (Revelation 12:11).

4

Civil Disobedience
Daniel & the Intersection of Allegiances

RYAN BELL

The political scene in Daniel 6 should be very familiar to us. It should also present some stark challenges to our discipleship.

Daniel did not go to Babylon seeking power. To the contrary, he was deported, taken as a slave from Judah. Upon arriving in Babylon, Daniel was chosen for special training and ultimately a place in the Babylonian government. Through the years Daniel successfully walked the fine line between his allegiance to the God of his fathers and his duty to serve the foreign rulers to whom God had sent him. It would have been easy for Daniel to bend under the pressure to conform. From the very beginning his traditions were challenged and his loyalty tested. Daniel never wavered. He remembered who he was and to whom he owed primary allegiance.

Now, after a regime change and in a time of political tension, Daniel was chosen to be chief of staff in Darius's administration. Not surprisingly, the opposition pulled out all the stops. They set traps. I imagine video surveillance, wiretaps, and secret agents ordered to follow Daniel and catch him in a compromising situation. None of these strategies worked, and the Bible testifies, "They could find no corruption in him, because he was trustworthy and neither corrupt nor negligent" (Dan. 6:4). It's almost impossible to imagine such a situation today!

Not giving up without a fight, Daniel's political rivals developed a new plan. "We shall not find any ground for complaint against this Daniel unless we find it in connection with the law of his God," they concluded (see v. 5). If you can't catch him doing something wrong, catch him doing something right. Darius, King of Media, flattered by the governors' proposal did what all self-respecting dictators do—he demanded absolute allegiance from the citizens on pain of death.

Daniel had been here before. This kind of conflict of allegiance was typical for a Jew living and working in a pagan empire. When Shadrach, Meshach, and Abednego (or, if you have kids, Rack, Shack, and Benny) were threatened with death in the face of similar demands, they remained loyal to God and defied the king. Even before that, Daniel placed himself in jeopardy by refusing to eat the king's food, which would have violated his Jewish customs.

Now, similarly:

> Although Daniel knew that the document had been signed, he continued to go to his house, which had windows in its upper room open toward Jerusalem, and to get down on his knees three times a day to pray to his God and praise him just as he had done previously. The conspirators came and found Daniel praying and seeking mercy before God (vv. 10-11).

The Demand For Total Allegiance

Today, in dozens of regimes around the world, this sort of absolute allegiance is demanded. Christians give their lives because they choose to follow Daniel's example. The story of his faithfulness inspires the radical way in which they practice their faith.

In the United States, up until very recently, this type of total allegiance has not been demanded. Many Americans have given it without being asked, but most have embraced the genius of America—the freedom to place other allegiances first. However in this post-9/11 world, more is being required. Dissenters are branded "unpatriotic" and freedoms are discarded in exchange for promises of security.

Even Christians have forgotten that safety is not the first consideration. In fact, God never calls his people to a life of safety. Jesus said exactly the opposite—"If anyone would come after me, he must deny himself and take up his cross and follow me" (Mark 8:34). In the famous words of Dietrich Bonhoeffer, "When Christ calls a man, he bids him come and die."

Certainly, if this story teaches us anything it teaches us that this kind of loyalty is what God requires. Nothing—not our safety, not patriotism, not even a denomination—deserves our absolute loyalty. The minute we begin making compromises like this we are heading down the path of idolatry. It may not be a ninety-foot image on the plain of Dura, but to the degree that it is more subtle, it is more insidious and dangerous.

Piety Goes Public

As a pastor, I've been asked why Daniel had to pray at his window. After all, God would hear his prayer just the same if he simply closed the shutters. That way he could practice his religion and spare his life.

As I reflect on that question, I realize it's a little like asking Rosa Parks why she didn't just move to the back of the bus. After all, the seats were just the same in the back. She could get a ride to her destination and save herself the trouble of all those angry white folks. I think Ms. Parks would say, "It's the principle of the thing!" She had had enough of the evil institution of racism and she wasn't going to take it anymore, even at the cost of her life. Thanks to heroic leaders like Martin Luther King, Jr., and Mahatma Gandhi we have terminology for this behavior—we call it civil disobedience, nonviolent resistance, or peaceful protest.

Whatever you call it, it is an oft-neglected part of Christian witness in the Western world. Yet it remains part of the holiness that is God's vision for his people. I grew up thinking that Daniel's decision had mostly to do with his personal piety, and certainly that dimension is there in the story. But if that was the main point he most certainly should have closed the shutters. The fact that he prayed publicly in spite of the decree points to the fact that public piety was primary.

What's more, this story teaches us that there are profound intersections of personal and public holiness. One of those intersections is worship. The notion of worship as public witness is perhaps nowhere more powerfully demonstrated than here in Daniel 6. The significance of this cannot be overstated, especially for Christians for whom prayer has been reduced to personal piety and practiced in the privacy of one's own home. That is the formative power of this narrative and something that should not be lost on Christians living in America and elsewhere in a world of nationalistic ideologies.

> "And I saw another angel fly in the midst of heaven, having the everlasting gospel to preach unto them that dwell on the earth, and to every nation, and kindred, and tongue, and people, Saying with a loud voice, Fear God, and give glory to him; for the hour of his judgment is come"(Revelation 14:6-7).

5
God Bless Afghanistan
The Rhetoric of Justice in the Sermon on the Plain

KEITH AUGUSTUS BURTON

This chapter is drawn from Dr. Burton's Black History Month Lecture, presented at Garrett-Evangelical Theological Seminary, Northwestern University, in Evanston, Illinois during February 2002, soon after the beginning of U.S.-led military action in Afghanistan.

I will always remember that touching moment after the terrorist attack on September 11, 2001. In the wake of the tragedy, members of Congress made a rare show of unity. Temporarily suspending the domestic war over the state of the economy and election fraud, the majority and minority leaders voiced unswerving support for the President and his idealistically termed "Operation Enduring Freedom." At the conclusion of the speeches, spontaneity took over. As if a mass choir, our elected officials burst into song,

> God bless America, land that I love, stand beside her and
> guide her
> Through the night with the light from above
> From the mountains, to the prairies, to the ocean white
> with foam
> God bless America, my home sweet home.

Although not an American, I could not help but get caught up in the emotion of the moment.

Other nations have their incantations that they hope would attract God's attention to the exclusion of others. Great Britain, the land of my birth, chants, "Land of hope and glory, mother of the free... God who made us mighty, make us mightier yet." "God save the gracious queen, long live the noble queen, God save the queen." The small island of Jamaica which nurtured my immediate ancestors pleads, "Eternal Father, bless our land, guard us with thy mighty hands, keep us free from evil powers, be our light through countless hours...." And the African National Congress cries from the depths of its soul, "Lord bless Africa, may her horn rise high up, hear thou our prayers and bless us." Every nation and people wants God on its side. Even in the midst of oppressive segregation, when the Johnson brothers penned an anthem around which my African-American brothers and sisters could rally, they concluded not only with a pledge to be "true to our God," but also to be "true to our native land."[1]

God Bless America

As we reflect on the terrible tragedy of 9/11, how is the Christian in America supposed to react? Do we join the majority who have overwhelmingly endorsed the government's violent response? After all, we do benefit from the military prowess of the armed forces. And don't we have a right to defend ourselves against unprovoked, unwarranted attacks from those who are "jealous of our freedoms." What should our response be to the enemy? What does justice demand in a situation like this?

Secretary of State Powell and National Security Advisor Condeleeza Rice would have us believe that President Bush is right in his reckless promise not only to inflict destructive wrath upon terrorists, but upon the countries that "host" terrorists (the newly adopted policy of a nation that keeps the Irish Republican Army viable and uses the Central Intelligence Agency to train "resistance" movements in the fine art of terrorism, including germ warfare). National justice is often governed by a warped form of *lex talionis*. In it's pure form, *lex talionis* demands that the offender receives just retribution for the crime. The American version of *lex talionis* goes many steps further in its effort to permanently remove the offender and preemptively scare any would be offenders. Hiroshima, Nagasaki, Haiti, Grenada, and Desert Storm gave us front row seats to the avenging wrath of a furious nation with bigger guns than the rest of the world.

Biblical justice comes in a different mold than the machismo mentality inherent in the *lex talionis*. Of course the holiness code that served as the constitution of the Israelite nation contains sections prescribing the penalty for capital offences. However, the vision of a just society heralded by the classical prophets elevates a world that is absent from rivalry and war. A global community where nations "study war no more." An arsenal-free world where swords, spears, bayonets, M16s, F16s, Stealth bombers, smart bombs, dumb bombs, anthrax, and cruise missiles have been permanently erased from the human memory. Indeed, this vision of a just society is central to the liberating teaching of Messiah Jesus.

Nowhere in the New Testament is the practical demand of this vision more plain than in the Gospel of Luke. Mary prophecies, "[God] has scattered the proud in the imagination of their hearts, he has put down the mighty from their thrones, and exalted those of low degree; he has filled the hungry with good things, and the rich he has sent away empty" (Lk 1:52-53). The angel tells the shepherds, "I bring you good news of a great joy which will come to *all* the people...." (Lk 2:10). Simeon can depart with hopeful peace, because "my eyes have seen the salvation which God has prepared in the presence of *all* peoples, a light for revelation to the Gentiles, and for glory to God's people, Israel" (Lk 2:30-32).

When responding to inquiries about practical manifestations of piety, John the Baptist advises his audience, "the one who has two coats, let him share with the one who has none; and the one who has no food, let him do likewise....Don't use your position to exploit others and get rich....Don't get corrupted by power, and live within your means" (Lk 3:11-14). Even Jesus' provocative homecoming sermon in Nazareth is under girded by the Isaianic vision of global emancipation: "The Spirit of the Lord is upon me, because he has anointed me to preach good news to the poor. He has sent me to proclaim release to the captives and recovery of sight to the blind, to set at liberty those who are oppressed, to proclaim the acceptable year of the Lord" (Lk 4:18-19).

From a Christian perspective, the creation of a just society demands pre-emptive pro-action rather than destructive reaction. In one section of the Sermon on the Plain, Jesus promotes eight rules of engagement that are intended to transform attitudes:

> But I say to you who are listening: Love your enemies, do good to those who hate you, bless those who curse you, pray for those who mistreat you. To the person who strikes you on the cheek, offer the other as well, and from the person who takes away your coat, do not withhold your tunic either. Give to everyone who asks you, and do not ask for your possessions back from the person who takes them away (Lk 6:27-31).

Of course, since our government is not driven by the desire or the mandate to conduct itself according to Christian principles, I don't expect the National Security Council to embrace this passage as a mission statement. However, I do expect Christian leaders to be that corrective moral voice in society. Somebody has to set John Ashcroft straight. In his recent address to the National Religious Broadcasters Conference (February 18, 2002) the Attorney General presumptuously proclaimed, "America is protecting God's gift of freedom." Ashcroft seems to believe that it is God that needs America, and not America that needs God.

Many Christians in America have obviously forgotten that God is not a territorial God. There seems to be a notion that God has a special relationship with this nation. Tragedies like the recent one help to bring out a person's true colors. On a daily basis, Dave Ramsey, talk show host and founder of Financial Peace University, claims, "The only way to financial peace is to live daily with the Prince of Peace, Christ Jesus." Yet, in the wake of the disaster on September 11th, he used his show as a vehicle of war, calling down merciless vengeance upon Afghanistan. So-called born again Christian and nationally syndicated Mike Gallagher continues to spew his racist rhetoric, publically supporting prejudiced behavior towards non-white people suspected to be terrorists, and callings for "a life for a life." He seems to have forgotten that the last two terrorists who destroyed the government building in Oklahoma were not named Hussein and bin Laden but McVeigh and Nichols.

Even popular Christian prophets have buckled under this new wave of nationalism. After the tragedy, religious-right spokesperson, Pat Robertson, stood upon his soap box and proclaimed that the event indicated the judgment of God upon a nation blighted with moral decay. However, after being rebuked as unpatriotic by fellow Republicans, his backbone jellied under pressure and he publicly recanted.

Though a longstanding critic of American hypocrisy, even the Seventh-day Adventist Church has buckled under nationalistic pressure. The world headquarters is doing its best to play down statements about judgment on capitalist America made by major church prophet, Ellen G. White as they send out public relations literature stating that God could not possibly be angry with America.

Our Black religious leaders also appear to have dropped the ball on this one. Many of our Black leaders are basking in the abundance of capitalistic wealth and are hesitant to speak out publicly against global injustice and national retribution. We need a Martin Luther King whose popularity was challenged by his own associates when he dared to think globally and decry the evil motives behind the Vietnam War, and charged America with being the "greatest purveyor of violence in the world today."[2] We need a Mohammed Ali who can temper the uncontrolled patriotic zeal of almost 50% of African-Americans

53

with his reminder that "No Viet-cong ever called me *nigger."* We need a Malcolm X who can agitate the conscience of those of our people confined to reservations known as public housing with his rejoinder, "I am not an American, I am a victim of Americanism." Where are the Black prophets in this *kairos?*

We have quickly forgotten that this is not a true democracy. How can you justify a system where a disproportionate number of the elected government officials have seven figure bank accounts and six figure salaries? How can you justify a system where the wishes of the majority are not honored, and in a bid to create a dynasty, a family can am*bush* an election? How can you justify a system that has forced U.S. companies to pay $8 billion in reparations to survivors of a holocaust that occurred on foreign soil, but has still not compensated the survivors of slavery with the forty acres of arable land and a mule? Does a nation concerned about justice walk out of a conference on racism and state sponsored terrorism in Durban, South Africa?

We have quickly forgotten that freedom and liberty are illusionary metaphors in this country. Even as our leaders call for a protection of our civil rights and freedoms, have we forgotten what it means to be *driving while black*? Have we forgotten about racial profiling? Have we forgotten the plight of Sung Ho Woo who was accused of espionage simply because he is Chinese?

Have we forgotten why we need Affirmative Action? Whose rights are we protecting anyhow? Is it the right of Enron executives to withdraw millions of dollars from a sunken ship without any government retribution? Is it the right for the Disney Corporation to fire its president after one year and reward him with a 10 million dollar severance package? Is it the rights of the multi-national corporations who – in the name of capitalism — exploit the citizens of Afghanistan, China, Mexico, Pakistan, Egypt, and other nations we deplore? Are we protecting the freedom to indulge in luxurious goods — a freedom that is enabled and sustained by our "third world" slaves?

While our currency is engraved with the words "In God We Trust," there is absolutely nothing in this country's European history that can verify this to be in truth the practice of our government. In every era of European and American history, a group of people has been victimized and exploited. The trusting natives who understood that national boundaries are humanly contrived illusions that restrict the movement of God's creatures on this wonderful planet—these natives were deprived of their freedom and to this day many are restricted to landlocked reservations. The African was abducted from foreign shores and is still the only person with American citizenship who does not have the perpetual right to vote. Japanese Americans felt the sting of the government when they were unlawfully detained during the second world war while German and Italian Americans walked free, even as Hitler and Mussolini terrorized the world. Most recently, it is the Hispanics who are being exploited as the new servant class in this nation driven by capitalistic aspirations.

America claims to be a Christian nation. However, there is no such thing as a Christian nation. There is absolutely no earthly nation upon which God has garnered his approval. Even Israel whom God had handpicked and protected failed to represent Him. If the chosen Israel was not able to receive his blessings, what makes us think that our law-breaking, sin-struck, vice-filled societies can? No earthly nation can claim to represent God.

True followers of Christ, I maintain, should not be mesmerized by the hypnotic hype of the moment, but need to stay sober and vigilant as "the adversary walks around like a roaring lion seeking whom he may devour." Those who call themselves children of God need to acknowledge that God does not have an American ZIP code. God is a universal God who is not confined to national boundaries.

In spite of these realities, many of us have bought into the nationalistic propaganda. We've adopted a juvenile attitude towards foreigners. We are xenophobic. We applaud when

President Bush taunts, "If you mess with one American, you mess with all of us." We feel no shame when self-righteous Donald Rumsfeld taunts God with his declaration, "God have mercy on Afghanistan, because we won't."

Many of us have bought into what Robert Jewett calls *The Captain America Complex*.[3] We've turned into a nation of vigilantes and are forming our own misguided posses. Since the terrorist attacks, assaults against people with Asian characteristics have rocketed. Many people are viewing our Moslem brothers and sisters as the enemy. Say what you may, but when the President has set his sights on Iraq, Somalia, the Philippines, and Palestine, anyone can see that he is following in the footsteps of the crusaders. As far as Bush and his cabinet are concerned, the prophetic voices in Islam must be silenced. America even disrespects nations that have extended an olive leaf. A recent report in *USA Today* told of the United States' refusal to mandate that their female soldiers in Saudi Arabia wear the *abaya*, even though Saudi Arabian law dictates that all women should wear the *abaya* regardless of religion.[4] As we move with bigoted blindness, Croatian president, Stipe Mesic, had to remind us that if Islam is to be blamed for the events of September 11, Christianity must be blamed for the holocaust.

Yet, our xenophobia has led us to pounce on a vulnerable scapegoat—Afghanistan. The term "Taliban" has become synonymous with all that is evil. By now, we have all heard about the atrocities of the Taliban in Afghanistan. We have seen documentaries about how they suppress their women and restrict education. This is the backwards, uneducated, unchristian, undemocratic enemy that needs to be annihilated.

Bush keeps referring to this as a fight between good and evil. Only evil people can carry out terrorist activities. While I acknowledge that the Taliban and Osama bin Laden are indeed sponsors of evil, I maintain that many of us have short term memory. We have forgotten that state-sponsored terrorist activities took place unabated for centuries in the United States of America. We have forgotten the millions from the so-called

Gold Coast, taken to a strange land. We have forgotten the millions who died in the middle passage. We have forgotten the hundreds of thousands who froze to death in frigid shacks when they encountered their first winter. We have forgotten those beaten to death by vindictive masters. We have forgotten those who were lynched during Jim Crow. We have forgotten the tens of thousands of political prisoners who are behind bars because their limited budget kept them on crack, while their wealthy white counterparts on cocaine are free to walk the streets.

We have forgotten that the terrorists Nathan Forest, Oliver North, Christopher Columbus, and George Custer, are revered as national heroes. We have forgotten the state-sponsored terrorism during the riots in Watts and Chicago. We have forgotten the fire hoses; the Edmund Pettus bridge; the Tuskegee experiment; the disproportionate number of Blacks among the "grunts" in the armed forces. We have forgotten the Trail of Tears and the Cherokees' forced exodus to Oklahoma. We have forgotten the CIA involvement in bringing down foreign governments and its recent covert sponsorship of Osama bin Laden himself. We have forgotten how the U.S.-controlled International Monetary Fund has destroyed economies through Africa and the Caribbean with its notoriously evil lending practices.

No nation is immune from committing evil acts. The American government is as treacherous as the Taliban. The survivors of No Gun Ri and the memory of My Lai remind us that Uncle Sam's troops have the potential to inflict the same atrocities as the programmed destroyers under the command of Pol Pot, Idi Amin, or Adolph Hitler. The British government is as deceitful as the ruling family of Saudi Arabia. The Jamaican government is as cutthroat as the Taiwanese. All nations inhabit and propagate evil. Former Yugoslav leader, Slobadan Milosovic, had to remind us from his trial at the Hague, "You in the west with your nice homes and radar skirting bombers, you too are bloodied."[5] Indeed, it is in recognition of America's role

57

in world evil that U.S. Representative Barbara Lee of California cast the sole vote against aggressive reaction to the September 11th attack, as she charged the nation with hypocrisy. She realized that before we move to take the splinter out of another person's eye, we must remove the log from our own.

God Bless Afghanistan

Although we know the negatives in our nation's history, as creatures of culture and citizens of countries, we still tend to wish blessings upon our place of domicile. We still wish that our nation will be insulated and isolated from all external evil. And so our leaders continue to repeat the three-word prayer, "God bless America."

Bin Laden has given an indirect response to this prayer in one of the tapes he sent to an Arabic television station. Some heard it as a threat, but it is actually a recognition of fact. Bin Laden declared, "America will not experience security until the world experiences security." The truth is, America will *never* be blessed in isolation. A picture of a truly blessed land is painted by the ancient Hebrew prophets who describe a land where "swords are transformed into plow shares and spears into pruning hooks." A blessed nation has no need for an army, for Yahweh Sabaoth is its protector. A blessed nation has no need for a National Security Czar, for El Shaddai patrols its borders. A blessed nation has no need to fear terrorist attacks, for it can truly say "In God we trust."

In fact, if indeed God were to pour out his blessings on individual nations, and he had to choose between America and Afghanistan, Jesus in Luke 6:20-23 gives us a clear indicator who the recipients of blessing would be. He declares: "Blessed are you poor," "blessed are you who are hungry," "blessed are you who weep," "blessed are you when men hate you." When one examines the condition of the two countries in light of the Sermon on the Plain, Afghanistan is more poised for God's blessing than is America. Afghanistan is one of the poorest countries on the face of the earth, and has been ravaged by decades of unrest and civil war after release from English domination. Death and starvation are commonplace. The infant mortality rate is seriously high. Few people live past the age of fifty. Poverty, famine, mourning, and ridicule are the order of the day. I submit again, if God were into the nation blessing business, then surely Afghanistan would be poised for a blessing—Divine justice demands it!

Conversely, if God were to pour out his wrath on individual nations and placed America and Afghanistan in front of him, guess who the most likely candidate would be? In Luke 6:24-26, Jesus warns: "woe to you that are rich," "woe to you that are full now," "woe to you that laugh now," "woe to you when all people speak well of you." When compared to the rest of the world, America boasts the material manifestations that some confuse with the blessings of God. The GDP is high. Most can access health care. The infant mortality rate is low. Life expectancy is high. Since the Civil War, the country has not experienced war on its soil. People on welfare receive more money in a month that a pastor in Uganda earns in a year. The food that is thrown away on a daily basis is enough to wipe out world hunger. We have entertainment machines and gadgets in every room of the house. The whole world marvels after our success. We see these as symbols of blessing, but God looks at our selfishness and proclaims a curse on the system – Divine justice demands it!

Many Christians have lost sight of the social implications of Christianity. From its very inception, Christianity has decried the evils of capitalistic greed. In fact, in Revelation 18, the prophet decries the capitalistic system as he announces the fall of Babylon. When Babylon falls, the stock brokers and CEOs of the multinationals weep and wail. Ziggy Marley is correct in his observation that the major reason for the judgment upon Babylon stems from its pleasure in "conquering the poor and oppressing the underprivileged." A few days after September 11, one of my colleagues shared a statement with me that was written almost 100 years ago by Ellen G. White,

On one occasion, when in New York City, I was in the night season called upon to behold buildings rising story after story toward heaven. These buildings were warranted to be fireproof, and they were erected to glorify their owners and builders. Higher and still higher these buildings rose, and in them the most costly material was used....

As these lofty buildings went up, the owners rejoiced with ambitious pride that they had money to use in gratifying self and provoking the envy of their neighbors. Much of the money that they thus invested had been obtained through exaction, through grinding down the poor. They forgot that in heaven an account of every business transaction is kept; every unjust deal, every fraudulent act, is there recorded....

The scene that next passed before me was an alarm of fire. Men looked at the lofty and supposedly fire-proof buildings and said: "They are perfectly safe." But these buildings were consumed as if made of pitch. The fire engines could do nothing to stay the destruction. The firemen were unable to operate the engines.[6]

While reading this statement, I was especially drawn to the sections denouncing capitalist exploitation. Indeed, the World Trade Center was constructed and maintained by the wealth of exploited people. The diamonds and gold of southern Africa and India. The oil of Afro-Asia. The bauxite of Jamaica and Venezuela. On September 11, America reaped a small portion of what it had sown, and according to the biblical mandate of Divine Justice, if she continues sowing seeds of terror around the globe, the worst is yet to come.

I dare not minimize the multi-faceted impact of the recent acts of atrocity. I dare not trivialize the horror of Satan's ability to beguile the gullible in the name of faith. I dare not remind America that "chickens come home to roost." But at the same time, as Christians, we need to wake up to the reality that human suffering did not start on September 11, 2001. "Tragedy" is not a concept that was recently invented. The 3000+ lives are but a fraction of those who suffer globally as a result of the Devil's terrorist activities.

When a recent hurricane ravaged havoc in the Caribbean, skipped the Carolinas and hit South America, one newscaster had pleasure in announcing the "good news." "Good news" because American lives had been spared. Good news from whose perspective? When the lone survivor thanks God for saving him from disaster when others have lost their lives, does he think that God is smiling? Does God only weep when American lives are lost? Is He not concerned about the thousands of Afghans who have been slaughtered by the Taliban. Is he not appalled at the hosts of Kurds who suffer at the hands of Saddam Hussein. Is he not moved when US missiles end the lives of Iraqi and Afghan children who are relegated to *collateral damage*? Does he not ache when millions of children in India, Somalia, Sudan, Poland, and Romania die from starvation? Does he not weep when the masses in Uganda, Kenya, Zimbabwe, Azania, and Botswana are stricken by the human-immuno-deficiency virus? On September 11, horror came closer to home, but we experienced just a little of what millions around the globe experience on a daily basis.

As I surveyed national anthems in preparation for this presentation, I came across one with a very interesting second verse:

> Our revolutionary homeland is now in the hands of the workers.
> The inheritance of lions now belongs to the peasants.
> The age of tyranny has passed, the turn of the laborers has come.
> We want peace and brotherhood between the peoples of the world.
> We demand more freedom for all who toil.
> We want bread for them, we want houses and clothes.

If only all national anthems celebrated the return of wealth to the masses. If only all national anthems championed the rights of the people over tyrannous corporations. If only all national anthems permeated nationalistic borders and embraced the vision of global peace. If only all national anthems were like this one — the one adapted by Afghanistan in 1978.

61

Conclusion

In his recent address at the annual conference of the Nation of Islam, before he quoted Galatians 3:28, Louis Farakhan had to remind his Christian listeners, "If you are a part of nationalism, you are not Christian." As we reflect on the biblical teaching on the blessings of God, I challenge all Christians to free themselves from the noose of nationalism and connect with God's global community. Lets never get to the point where we believe that only America deserves God's blessings. Indeed, the credo of Christianity is found in John 3:16: "For God so loved *the world.*"

When we start thinking globally, our prayer will not simply be "God bless America," but as we reflect on the millions of lives that are being eternally altered as a result of United States foreign policy, we will pray, "God bless those who suffer in Afghanistan, Iraq, Pakistan, India, Zimbabwe, Kenya, Azania, Botswana, Nigeria, Ghana, and in the uttermost parts of the world."

Even as we are being drawn by the magnet of nationalistic nepotism, Nebuchadnezaar's vision in Daniel 2 helps us to see things in their true perspective. Nebucahdnezaar was given a vision of the successive kingdoms that precede the Kingdom of God, but forgot how the vision ended. Instead of leaning on God's providence, Nebuchadnezaar built an image of gold, "God bless Babylon!" But Babylon fell. The vision had not ended.

Darius came after and built an image of silver, "God bless Persia!" But Persia fell. The vision had not ended.

Alexander the Great came after, and built an image of bronze, "God bless Greece!" But Greece fell. The vision had not ended.

Octavius Augustus came after and built an image of iron, "God bless Rome!" But Rome fell. The vision had not ended.

Charlemagne, Ferdinand and Isabel, Henry the Navigator, James I, Napolean Bonaparte, and a host of others were the tentacles of Europe that embraced the globe and tried to build an image of iron and clay, "God bless Europe!" But Europe is still divided, and the vision has not ended.

Then came Washington, Lafayette, Jefferson, Hancock, Lincoln, Roosevelt, Kennedy, Nixon, Reagan, Clinton, and Bush, who have built an image of false security, "God bless America!" But the vision has still not been fulfilled.

The vision will not be fulfilled until the stone is hewn from the mountain and crushes all earthly powers and potencies. This is the event that will put an end to all nationalistic pride once and for all. It's the event that will completely obliterate all ethnic and social distinctions. I submit that the only kingdom worthy of God's blessing is represented by that stone. I'm talking about the blessed kingdom that succeeds all earthly kingdoms. In Revelation 11:15, John speaks of its inauguration as the time when, "The kingdom of the world has become the kingdom of our Lord and his Messiah." The only blessing that can bring healing to a hurt nation is the blessing that comes from God's antiseptic judgment—a judgment that rids the world of evil forces and influences.

As we prepare for the final universal blessing, God does not call us to pledge allegiance to a nationalistic flag; he needs us to pledge allegiance to the international cross; where the hungry find food, where the weary find rest, where the bereaved find peace, where the impoverished find satisfaction. He calls us to pronounce his blessings to suffering and searching people in every nation. That's why I say, "God bless Afghanistan, and Iraq, and Iran, and Israel, and the PLO, and Egypt, and Croatia, and Trinidad, and Guyana, and China, and France, and, yes, God bless America."

6

Second Advent Hope
The Presence of the Future

KENDRA HALOVIAK

I saw a new heaven and a new earth; for the first heaven and the first earth had passed away, and the sea was no more. And I saw the holy city, the new Jerusalem, coming down out of heaven from God, prepared as a bride adorned for her husband. And I heard a loud voice from the throne saying,
"See, the home of God is among mortals.
He will dwell with them as their God;
they will be his peoples,
and God himself will be with them;
he will wipe every tear from their eyes.
Death will be no more;
mourning and crying and pain will be no more, for the first things have passed away."
And the one who was seated on the throne said, "See, I am making all things new" (Rev. 21:1-5a).*

This amazing vision at the end of the book of Revelation is about a renewed, re-created world. The vision is so vast that it overwhelms our imaginations; it astonishes, captivates, and moves us. Thus, this vision of a future, renewed realm is able to transform our lives now in our present existence.[1] As a pastor I have especially seen this transforming vision "arrive" at funerals, and I've watched people with hearts breaking with grief imagine themselves reunited with their loved one in a new, remade earth. Somehow there is a power in this vision that transforms our present pain. Even though it does not eliminate all the heartache of the present, it makes facing another day possible.

Vision

Everyone called her "Aunt Clara." She was one of the 18 residents of the Hillhaven Nursing Home in Silver Spring, Maryland, where at the age of 16, I worked part time as a nurses' aide. Our youngest resident was 79, our oldest, 101. Aunt Clara was almost 90. She was a delight to care for. Easygoing and kind, she had a wonderful sense of humor.

One evening, while working the 3/11 shift, I noticed that Aunt Clara had fallen asleep in her chair. I went over to gently wake her by placing my hand on hers. As I got closer, something caused me to pause just before my hand reached hers. With my hand right next to hers, I noticed the huge contrast between them. I remember thinking, someday my hand will look like Aunt Clara's; someday I will need a young woman to help me get ready for bed.

That evening, standing next to Aunt Clara, I glimpsed the future, imagining myself at 90. My "vision of the future" indeed caused me to think quite differently about the present.

A glance into the future transformed the way I saw the present.

In a much more dramatic way, John, the seer of Patmos, had the same kind of experience. He did not merely see the aging of an individual, he saw the aging and the restoring of the cosmos! He looked into the future, and what he saw transformed his present.

The future became so real, so present in his own experience that it changed not only the way he saw the world but how he responded to that world. It transformed, too, the way he shared his faith—the way he called others to view the world.

While John's contemporaries looked out at a world dominated by the Roman Empire, a world where power won all arguments, John's vision allowed him to see a different reality. John might have seen only a world in which those who proclaimed Jesus were a small, seemingly insignificant sect, apparently on the verge of extinction. That was the "reality" others saw in that turbulent first century. But they didn't have the vision.

Instead, this banished man of Patmos, old and alone and soon to die, saw a world where those who proclaim Jesus as the Christ would stand victorious. Instead of a world where Caesar was lord and Christ seemed little to nothing, John saw a world where the holy God sits upon the throne with "every creature in heaven and on earth, and under the earth" paying Him unbridled homage (Rev. 5:13).

After John's commission to write to the seven churches of Asia Minor and the seven letters that follow in chapter three, the first words of Revelation 4 read:

> After this I looked, and there in heaven a door stood open! And the first voice, which I had heard speaking to me like a trumpet, said, "Come up here, and I will show you what must take place after this."

Typically apocalyptic literature begins with the seer being taken off in vision through distant lands and strange eras, with an emphasis on the huge gap between God's realm and our human, earthly existence. However, the book of Revelation is written from the perspective of one who believes in *Emmanuel* (God with us!).

In other words, this is a Christian apocalypse. This book about the future includes a God who entered human history in the past and whose spirit continues to be with the churches. This book about the future is expressed in scenes that John's audience can understand—they are scenes of worship!

Worship

In verses 2-8, John attempts to describe the indescribable throne of God. He says that it appears like jasper and carnelian, and has a rainbow that looks like an emerald. There are strange creatures with eyes all around. Then he hears the familiar sounds of worship: "Holy, holy, holy, the Lord God the Almighty, who was and is and is to come."

Instead of a future time and a totally unfamiliar realm, John knows he is in the presence of God, in a worship scene like that of Isaiah and the prophets before him. John watches, and then participates. And through his account of the vision, he invites his readers to do the same; for worship scenes invite participation.

Such worship surrounds each key moment in Revelation. This book, so strange and troubling at times, is full of worship scenes. Sixteen songs fill its pages, along with other aspects of worship, such as prayers, offerings, and proclamations.[2] Even when judgment occurs, there is singing! The frightening scenes of warning and judgment are surrounded by images of the redeemed singing and celebrating.

The worship scenes are not only relegated to some future time; they involve the present. When we enter the worship scenes, we experience the presence of the future. When we enter the worship scenes, the future transforms our present lives.

Transformation

The first song in the book of Revelation is sung by the four living creatures day and night without ceasing: "Holy, holy, holy, the Lord God the Almighty, who was and is and is to come."

The only other time in Scripture that we hear the song "Holy, Holy, Holy" is in Isaiah 6, when the prophet Isaiah enters into a heavenly throne room scene. In the verses that surround this scene, especially those before it (Isaiah 1-5), God agonizes with Judah to turn from wickedness and to follow the holy God, who "shows himself holy by righteousness" (5:16).

In Revelation 4, John sees the worship of the holy God and, in the experience of worship, this God is present. God is not far removed in time and space, but present in worship. The One who is the Almighty, the One who is God of all time ("who was and is and is to come"), the God of all creation (verse 11), is present with John and with all believers who worship.

This God walks among the candlesticks and welcomes people into the throne room at the center of the universe. This song proclaims the presence of the future. All who sing Revelation's songs proclaim the experience of God in the present.

This song, like the experience of worship itself, calls us to embrace a different reality from the one we see. The name revelation means "unveiling" or "pulling back"; it implies a revelation of things as they really are, not as the world portrays them. Worship always calls us to see what is real, and then to act accordingly.

Such worship transforms our present. When we worship we anticipate a new heaven and a new earth. The future enters our present, and we live now as we will live in the future.

- **Because God's future will be an earth full of justice, worshipers seek *justice now*.**
- **Because God's future will bring peace on earth, worshipers act for *peace now*.**
- **Because God's future will be an earth with plenty for all, worshipers act to *end hunger now*.**
- **Because God's future will be existence without tears, worshipers act to *comfort* and to *heal now*.**
- **Because God's future will be life without death, worshipers act to *fight disease and death now*.**

As worshipers anticipate a new heaven and a new earth, the future enters their present, transforming it and calling them to live now as they will in a new heaven and a new earth.

Empowerment

One Easter Sabbath, while living in the San Francisco area, I attended a small Seventh-day Adventist Church in St. Helena, California. I walked in, having never been there before, and sat in an empty seat three rows from the front. Surrounding me on both sides were people in their 80s and 90s. I was reminded of the years I worked at Hillhaven.

When we stood together to sing "Christ the Lord Is Risen Today," I noticed the words as never before. I watched people who have lived decades longer than I have, and I listened to them enthusiastically sing, embodying in the present their hope for the future:

> Lives again our glorious king, Allelujah!
> Where, O death, is now thy sting? Allelujah!
> Once He died, our souls to save, Allelujah!
> Where's thy victory, boasting grave?, Allelujah!

After the pastor's powerful sermon, we prepared to sing the closing hymn.

The woman directly across the aisle from me was rubbing her knees. When the congregation stood to sing, I saw that it took her the entire first stanza to straighten out her arthritic knees. But she stood! She stood and she sang.

She has no idea how she blessed me. She embodied those singing before the throne, those whose hope in the future transforms their present. It was as if she were saying, I stand to sing now, because I will stand quickly and lightly some day. I look ahead through cataracts now, because I will see clearly someday. I worship and I sing now, because I will sing "Holy, holy, holy, the Lord God the Almighty, who was and is and is to come."

When we worship, our Advent hope about the future transforms our present experience.

*New Revised Standard Version used throughout this chapter.

70

7

A Brief History of Seventh-day Adventists in Time of War

RONALD OSBORN

The Seventh-day Adventist Church was founded by New England pacifists with intellectual and spiritual roots in the Radical or Anabaptist Reformation. In the first 60 years of the movement's history—from its organization in 1863 until the death of its prophetess, Ellen White, in 1915—Adventism may thus be seen as part of the same tradition of social and political dissent that gave rise to Quakers, Mennonites, and other religious communities committed to the ethics of nonviolence.

This commitment was both formally stated and rigorously practiced by early Adventists, many of whom believed that even touching a weapon was sinful. On May 23, 1865, the *Review and Herald* published a General Conference resolution "as a truthful representation of the views held by us from the beginning of our existence as a people, relative to bearing arms." The document—composed in the aftermath of a war that had caused many abolitionists to abandon their earlier pacifism—affirmed a legitimate role for the civil government, but declared that Adventists, as a people, are "compelled to decline all participation in acts of war and bloodshed as being inconsistent with the duties enjoined upon us by our divine Master toward our enemies and toward all mankind."

During the Spanish-American War of 1898-1899, Adventists thus emerged as outspoken critics of America's imperial foreign policy. In opposition to other prominent churches that embraced the war as a Christianizing and civilizing campaign, they pointed to the glaring inconsistency of linking the cross with militarism of any sort. "Christian love demands that its possessor shall not make war at all. 'Put up again they sword into his place,' is the word of the Author of Christianity, the embodiment of Christian love," thundered former army sergeant A. T. Jones. "Christianity is one thing; war is another, and far different thing. Christians are one sort of people; warriors are another and different sort of people." Percy Magan's *The Peril of the Republic*, rushed to print in 1899, similarly denounced American actions in the Philippines as mere "colonial greed and rapacious lust." Better, Magan argued, "for a few missionaries to lose their lives at the hands of heathen savages than for heathen savages to lose their lives at the hands of those calling themselves Christians."

The Adventist commitment to nonviolence during this period of the church's history was based not primarily upon concern for personal moral purity, but upon a systematic critique of America's revered institutions of power. According to the Adventist reading of the books of Daniel and Revelation, the United States could not fail as a nation so long as it remained true to its Republican and Protestant heritage. Yet the fact that America *would* eventually fail was a foregone conclusion. No nationalistic project could replace the divine plan to redeem humanity once and for all.

The creedalism and intolerance of the emerging Protestant empire—intent upon a new union of church and state—coupled with the social injustice implicit in the economic order, revealed the seeds of corruption eating at the heart of the American experiment. The United States, Ellen White, Joseph Bates, A. T. Jones and other Adventist pioneers declared, was the beast of

Revelation 13, a morally contradictory amalgamation of dragon and lamb-like qualities, who "doeth great wonders, so that he maketh fire come down from heaven on the earth, and deceiveth them that dwell on the earth by the means of those miracles." Even the best government in human history, these prophetic agitators insisted, had feet of clay.

II

From Ellen White's death in 1915 on, however, the Anabaptist ethos of the early church rapidly eroded. This was true in matters of ecclesiastical authority and biblical hermeneutics, but particularly with regard to the military and bearing arms. Following World War I the Adventist commitment to not taking life remained largely intact, yet church leaders increasingly described Adventists not as conscientious objectors but as "conscientious cooperators." The consensus of the new generation was that it was no longer the church's role to question the rightness of US military adventures or foreign policy so long as Adventist soldiers were allowed to continue in their peculiar commitment to Sabbath observance.

It was in this spirit of patriotic cooperation with the government that the Adventist Medical Cadet Corps was created in 1942. The Corps sought to prove that good Adventists were also "good Americans", eager and willing to serve in the military, albeit in noncombatant roles. The Corps thus helped to instill in a generation of young Adventists a love for military drill and bivouac, and the belief that it is honorable to serve power for the sake of order.

Unfortunately, these lessons could not be confined to one side of the Atlantic. During World War II Adventists proudly answered the call to duty in the United States, but also, and more disconcertingly, in Nazi Germany. While Protestant leaders of other denominations resisted fascism at considerable cost, there was no Adventist "Confessing Church", and up to the outbreak of the war Adventists even in the United States spoke of Hitler in positive terms as a fellow vegetarian concerned with matters of bodily hygiene. Whereas Adventist complicity in the Nazi onslaught, as well as the horrors of the Allied bombing campaign, might have sparked a recommitment to the nonviolent principles of the church's pioneers, Adventists from the 1950s on generally saw World War II as a vindication of violence for a just cause. The idea that loyalty to God and loyalty to the military were fully compatible became powerfully entrenched in the minds of many Adventists, particularly in North America.

Pockets of believers in Germany and other European countries retained the older ethics of nonviolence; and Russia's True and Free Adventists heroically resisted Soviet totalitarianism in defense of freedom and human rights. But these pacifists—whose convictions placed them firmly in the tradition of the church's founders—were disavowed and marginalized by presiding church officials. With a burgeoning network of health and educational institutions, and ambitious evangelistic campaigns around the world, maintaining good relations with government authorities now took precedence over prophetic and politically dangerous brands of dissent.

With more and more Adventist chaplains rising in military rank, the church was also already too deeply invested in the military as an institution to seriously question the logic of violence, or the rightness of American foreign policies abroad. The title of the Adventist chaplaincy's newsletter, *For God and Country*, revealed just how far pietism and patriotism had come to be wedded in the thinking of church leaders—and how far Adventists had come since Magan's *Peril of the Republic*.

III

By the time of the Vietnam War the Adventist position had thus fragmented into incoherency. Some Adventists evaded the draft, others entered as noncombatant medics, and others avoided direct military action by volunteering as human guinea pigs in Project White Coat - research program with links to the

US biological weapons laboratories at Fort Detrick, Maryland. During the war in Vietnam significant numbers of Adventists, encouraged by church officials to perform their patriotic duty according to "the dictates of their conscience", also picked up guns and, for the first time, began to kill according to the dictates of government planners.

In view of the vociferous Adventist response to the Spanish-American war, the silence of the church during the war in Indochina—and particularly the silence of those chaplains closest to the unfolding catastrophe—marked a stunning reversal in Adventism's historic identity, from fearless agitators to acquiescent mandarins of the state. Religious leaders of other faiths, such as Martin Luther King Jr., Thomas Merton, and Abraham Joshua Heschel, decried the war in unequivocal language. But through the carpet-bombing with napalm of hundreds of thousands of defenseless villagers; through the countless acts of brutality and depredation against unarmed civilians; through the dumping of millions of gallons of arsenic-based herbicides on Vietnamese crops and people—through all of this Adventists spoke not a word. In a tragically ironic twist, even as America acted increasingly like the beast Adventists had long proclaimed it to be, the prophetic movement proved an increasingly timid and sycophantic page at the dragon's side.

In the post-Vietnam era, thousands of Adventists voluntarily joined the U.S. armed forces as full combatants. Adventist chaplains were recruited to minister to these fighters "without passing judgment", which in turn encouraged more Adventists to enlist. With large numbers of Adventists on active duty, it is therefore not surprising that there was not a murmur of disapproval from the church in the 1970s and 1980s as the US military abetted Latin American juntas in the slaying of tens of thousands of impoverished peasants calling for land reform—many of them Christians who first heard about the Sabbath Jubilee from socially conscious Catholic priests.

During the 1990s and at start of the 21st century, the collapse of the historic Adventist ethic of nonviolence became apparent in other embarrassing ways. Early Adventist apocalyptic had led the movement to reject all acts of violence and bloodshed, but in Waco, Texas in 1993 one-time Adventists played out a new and violent apocalyptic nightmare on a compound bristling with weapons. In 1994 significant numbers of Adventist Hutus in Rwanda participated in the genocide of their Tutsi countrymen, including an estimated ten thousand Seventh-day Adventists. Through the 1990s — as Buddhist Nobel Peace Prize winner, Ang San Suu Kyi, attracted world attention in her nonviolent struggle against Burma's military dictatorship — hundreds of Karen Adventists, whose great-grandparents had been evangelized by legendary missionary Eric B. Hare, engaged in a campaign of guerrilla warfare against the Burmese army with the goal of creating an autonomous Karen nation. And in 2002 rival militias comprised largely of Adventists fought for control of the government of the Solomon Islands.

Yet while Adventists were quick to dismiss these events as tragic aberrations in the faith, they did not pause to consider the church's romance with more devastating forms of violence sanctified by the state. In 2002 a group of students from Oakwood College were arrested for gun-running between New York and Alabama. But the church saw no reason to disavow the voting records of Adventism's two most prominent gun-runners: US Congressmen Roscoe Bartlett of Maryland and Bob Stump of Arizona, who through the 1990s collected hefty sums from the National Rifle Association and military manufacturing lobbyists for helping to grease weapons sells at home and abroad.

The September 2001 terrorist attacks in the United States perhaps saw the final denouement of Adventism as a prophetic movement that could not be co-opted by nationalistic crusades. Amid the many heartfelt and sincere expressions of grief following the tragedy, churches from coast to coast reflexively wrapped themselves in the flag, no different from the rest of evangelical America. Sligo Church in Washington, DC featured a Veteran's Day service in which a military honor guard marched down the center aisle with bolt-action rifles gripped to their chests. And near the end of the American bombing campaign in Afghanistan, the General Conference organized a special weekend to honor the US military and send care packages overseas—not care packages to the afflicted Afghanis, but stuffed animals to U.S. bomber crews stationed at Diego Garcia Air Force Base in the Pacific Ocean. Little thought was given by the planners of the event to the history of American policy in the Middle East, or the estimated 3,400 Afghani civilians killed by US bombs – four hundred more innocent people than perished on September 11. Where Adventists once venerated those Protestant martyrs who died rather than betray their religious convictions, they would now honor US soldiers who kill at the bidding of their political masters.

As President George W. Bush promised to take his war against America's enemies to far-flung corners of the globe, one thing was certain: many Adventists would soon be shipping out to exotic lands, not as missionaries, but as warriors, assault rifles in hand.

8

Adventism's Peacemaking Heritage

DOUGLAS MORGAN

On April 6, 2005, Joel Klimkewicz, a Seventh-day Adventist incarcerated by the United States Marine Corps for his refusal to engage in killing, was freed from jail at Camp Lejeune, North Carolina, after serving nearly five months of a seven-month prison sentence. Early in 2003, several months after baptism as an Adventist, and only weeks after a second enlistment period began, the young marine became convinced that his faith commitment meant that he could not take human life. "My faith taught me that all human beings are part of one family, and I cannot take the life of a family member," Klimkewicz explained.[1]

Despite his offer to perform the dangerous task of clearing mines in Iraq, the Marine Corps court-martialed the noncombatant in December 2004. In addition to the seven-month imprisonment, the unusually harsh punishment deprived Klimkewicz of all pay and benefits and gave him a bad conduct discharge. Though his prison sentence was finally suspended after five-months, enabling him to rejoin his wife and three-year-old daughter and proceed with plans to study for gospel ministry at Southern Adventist University, his court-martial sentence was still in effect and under appeal as of this writing.

The nonviolent ethic that inspired a recent convert in the 21st century to endure a prison sentence for a principle has deep historical roots in Adventism. In a time of war, it becomes particularly useful to explore those roots. In so doing, we indeed find a heritage, not just of nonviolence, but of *peacemaking*.

"Biblical peace, or *shalom*, is a sweeping wholeness of life," writes Charles Scriven. "Where shalom prevails, freedom and safety prevail; justice overcomes oppression; plenty supplants poverty; joy defeats gloom and shame."[2] In addition to standing for nonviolence, the Adventist heritage includes other dimensions of peacemaking such as prophetic witness, and *shalom*-nurturing activism.

The examples in what follows are presented to illustrate the depth and authenticity of Adventism's peacemaking heritage, but not with the claim that they are definitive for the Adventist historical experience as a whole.

A Stand For Nonviolence

In the very years that the emerging Seventh-day Adventist movement was forging its organizational identity, the great national crisis of Civil War confronted them with the question of what their radical faith meant for the moral dilemma of war. The first conference (Michigan) organized in 1861, the year the war began. The first General Conference session began on May 20, 1863, two weeks after the stunning Confederate victory at Chancellorsville, and about six weeks before the great turning point marked by Union victories at Gettysburg and Vicksburg.

In the midst of the "fiery crisis" Adventists took a corporate stand for nonviolence, formulated through the interplay of three sometimes-conflicting influences: 1) convictions about scriptural imperatives, amplified by an identity as a prophetic minority commissioned to uphold "the commandments of God and the faith of Jesus;" 2) passionate opposition to slavery; and 3) pragmatic concerns for the survival of the fledgling movement.

We must recall the thoroughly radical dissent from the American religious and political mainstream that characterized early Seventh-day Adventism, which found its identity as "remnant" — a faithful minority bearing God's latter-day message — the third angel's messages — in the midst of pervasive apostasy.

For most Adventists, influenced by Scripture and by the Christian nonresistance movement led by social reformer William Lloyd Garrison, pacifism was a part of that radical faith that set them apart from the majority of Americans. The commitment to Christian nonresistance that had been espoused by the Millerite Adventist reformer Joshua V. Himes, as well as William Miller himself (according to Garrison), carried over to some extent into the post-1844 group that would become the Seventh-day Adventists and occasionally found expression in their publications during the 1850s. Moreover, a literal reading of the sixth commandment as well as the Sermon on the Mount fit well with the literal reading of the fourth commandment that the Seventh-day Adventists upheld. In this light, participation in military combat was a clear and simple violation of the sixth commandment and the teachings of Christ.[3]

At the same time, it was also important for the success of the fledgling church to show that its outsider identity did not entail rebellion against civil authority. Scripture also commands rendering due honor and subordination to civil authority. Thus, Adventists, who had not spread beyond the northern states at that point, sought ways to overcome suspicions that their deviation from the majority entailed disloyalty to the Union or sympathy for the Confederate rebellion.

The dilemma went deeper than simply than obedience to scriptural commandments about nonviolence vs. the imperatives of respectable citizenship. The Adventists' deep and outspoken opposition to slavery sharpened the dilemma. This abolitionist protest was a major theme in the Adventist dissent against America in this era of Protestant "empire" — both the Southern embrace of slavery and Northern complicity with it.

"God is punishing this nation for the high crime of slavery," Ellen White wrote in August 1861. "He has the destiny of the nation in His hands. He will punish the South for the sin of slavery, and the North for so long suffering its overreaching and overbearing influence."[4] As Roy Branson has shown, the *Review and Herald* joined in the abolitionist criticism of President Lincoln for failing to make emancipation a goal of the war, until the president began to do just that late in 1862.[5]

So, the dilemma: if they resisted military service out of faithfulness to scripture, they risked accusations of disloyalty, a severe government crackdown on their movement just as it was getting off the ground, and indirectly abetting the continuation of the slave system they so fiercely opposed. To join freely in armed combat, though, would make a mockery of their claim to be a remnant faithful to "the commandments of God and faith of Jesus." Their witness to the fourth commandment as well as the sixth would be compromised. Such a course would reduce conflict with the surrounding society but at the price of compromising the church's prophetic message and mission.

Here's how they worked through the dilemma. Initially, President Lincoln called upon the states to raise volunteer armies to fight the Confederate "insurrection." That created a certain pressure — the need for communities to meet quotas for bonuses to pay the volunteers. James White and John P. Kellogg participated on a Battle Creek committee for this purpose.[6]

But it was the growing possibility of a draft that created much more serious concerns, and prompted James White, the church's foremost organizer, to set forth a pragmatic line of thought in a *Review* editorial of August 1862 entitled, "The Nation." White reasoned that if Adventists were drafted, they would be well advised to submit, and the government would assume responsibility for any violations of the law of God.[7]

White's editorial sparked vigorous, extended debate in pages of the *Review* in which his position was attacked from all sides.

Some believers called for Adventist participation in the Union's "crusade against traitors"—one even fantasizing about an armed regiment of Sabbath-keepers that would "strike this rebellion a staggering blow." Others advocated thoroughgoing pacifism, including Henry Carver, who maintained "that under no circumstances was it justifiable in a follower of the Lamb to use carnal weapons to take the lives of his fellow-men." Adventists in Iowa petitioned the state legislature for recognition as a pacifist church.

White clarified in response that his controversial initial proposal was predicated on the following assumptions: 1) Adventists would not *volunteer* for service in the army; 2) that if drafted they would do their best to obtain Sabbath privileges and recognition as noncombatants—only if such efforts failed would moral culpability fall upon the government.

Then, just before the federal draft was instituted in March 1863, a testimony from Ellen White deftly set forth a position which avoided inflammatory posturing in any direction yet took a principled stand for nonviolence. The prophetess rebuked both the ill-considered bravado about resistance to the anticipated draft expressed by the Iowans zealous for a defiant pacifism, as well as the militant impulse to volunteer to take up arms for the Union's righteous cause. Adventists should not court martyrdom with provocative pronouncements, she cautioned. Yet, it remained the case that

> God's people...cannot engage in this perplexing war, for it is opposed to every principle of their faith. In the army they cannot obey the truth and at the same time obey the requirements of their officers.[8]

The guidance from Ellen White drew together and addressed the various conflicting influences that both motivated and unsettled Adventists in this time of crisis. They would take their stand for divine law, which meant commitment to a nonviolent ethic. Yet they should be prudent, avoiding rash moves that would unnecessarily provoke antagonism from the government. And, for similarly prudential reasons, but also because of their moral opposition to slavery, they would take every opportunity to show that they were not disloyal to the Union and were in fact advocates of the highest ideals for which their government stood.

The federal draft law enacted in March 1863 gave Adventists one way through the dilemma with its provisions for purchasing an exemption or providing a substitute. Though the hefty $300 commutation fee placed a financial strain on the church as it tried to raise the necessary funds for those who could not afford it, this provision made it possible to avoid messy confrontations with the government.

However, when Congress, in July 1864, restricted these options to conscientious objectors who were members of a recognized pacifist church, the Adventist leadership moved swiftly in seeking governmental recognition of their noncombatant position. Declaring themselves "a people unanimously loyal and anti-slavery" but unable to shed blood because of their views of the Ten Commandments and the teachings of the New Testament, they obtained an exemption from Provost Marshall General James Fry that gave them the option of either accepting assignment to hospital duty or care of freedmen or paying the $300 commutation fee.[9]

The success of their petition may obscure the fact that by thus bringing their nonconformity into the open, the little-known sect took the risk of its being rejected. Moreover, even with high level governmental recognition achieved, individual Adventist draftees frequently suffered denials, temporary imprisonment, threats of court-martial, and other forms of harassment when attempting to claim their right to alternative duty. Lack of understanding among officers about the Provost Marshall's ruling, prejudice against noncombatants, and poor communication all had a hand in causing the harassment to continue. However, the time had come to take a public stand.

Obtaining governmental recognition also had the effect of formalizing the church's own commitment to pacifism, which, though widely held, had not been formally delineated or expressed in a generally agreed upon form prior to the war. A resolution voted by the General Conference session of 1865 declared:

> While we thus cheerfully render to Caesar the things which the Scriptures show to be his, we are compelled to decline all participation in acts of war and bloodshed as being inconsistent with the duties enjoined upon us by our divine Master toward our enemies and toward all mankind.[10]

Further resolutions at the 1867 and 1868 sessions reaffirmed this position, suggesting that the issues of war and military service were of more than passing or marginal significance.[11]

Prophetic Witness

To take a public stand for nonviolence, and for the abolition of slavery, as the Adventists did — to build a community dedicated to these principles, is a profoundly political act; perhaps even the most powerful way for Christians to show political responsibility. Another dimension of peacemaking is to call for change in the surrounding society, the wider world beyond the community of believers. This may be termed "prophetic witness" because, in the tradition of the Hebrew prophets, it applies the word of the Lord to societal conditions — not denunciation or doomsaying for its own sake — but to provoke change.

While the Adventist church has too often we have been the "silent church" as reflected in the title of Zdravko Plantak's comprehensive study of human rights and social ethics in Adventism,[12] I want to offer two examples of peacemaking as "prophetic witness." The first, frequently overlooked, came in the era of the Spanish-American War, during which the United States began its emergence as a world power. Pacifism, and with it protest against war and militarism, appear more prominently at this time than any other in Adventist history.

The temptation to wrap the cross in the flag, to hijack Christian idealism for a nationalistic agenda, becomes particularly acute during wartime. Historian Sydney Ahlstrom points out that, during the period of the Spanish-American War and subsequent Filipino-American conflict, "patriotism, imperialism, and the religion of American Protestantism" stood in more "fervent coalescence than ever before."[13]

Dr. Frank Bristol, pastor of the Metropolitan Methodist Church in Washington, President William McKinley's place of worship, gave voice to this coalescence:

> Were the guns of Dewey and Sampson less providential than the ram's horns of Joshua, the lamps and pitchers of Gideon, or the rod of Moses? Were Manila and Santiago less providential in the history of freedom than Jericho and Ai? Is Christian civilization less providential than was Jewish barbarism?

Answering himself, the Rev. Bristol went on to intone, "If God ever had a peculiar people, He has them now" – namely, the American soldiers at Santiago who

> represent a manhood that has climbed century by century up the steeps of light and liberty, and now stands in sight of the glorified summits of the universal freedom and brotherhood of men.[14]

Ahlstrom, once again: "The churches reflected the American consensus" in favor of war in Cuba and Philippines and "then proceeded in the limited time available to convert the war into a crusade to rationalize imperialism as a missionary obligation."[15]

While the majority of churches joined a consensus that converted the war into a crusade for Christian civilization, Adventists spoke out against the "spirit of militarism" being fostered "right within the bosom of the church."[16] Preaching at the Battle Creek Tabernacle, General Conference President George Irwin declared, "We have no business whatever to become aroused and stirred by the spirit [of war] that is abroad in the land." He cited several passages from the Sermon on the Mount, affirming that these scriptures

> show what I believe is the position of the Christian in this conflict, and what are the teachings of our Lord and Master in regard to war and the spirit of what comes with war.[17]

After the United States annexed the Philippines in February 1899 and militarily suppressed an independence movement there, a wide array of voices in American society, including Adventists, charged the nation with imperialism. A.T. Jones, at this point editor of the *Review and Herald* as well as the *American Sentinel* and Percy T. Magan, a prominent Adventist educator and writer, were among the most vocal Adventist critics of the newly manifest American imperialism.[18]

In his *Peril of the Republic*, published in 1899 by the evangelical publishing house Fleming H. Revell, Magan extolled the principles of the Declaration of Independence and the Constitution as reflections of the divine government and near equivalent to the Word of God, and then decried the forcible annexation of the Philippines as "national apostasy" from those principles. In this embrace of imperialism, America was abandoning the "new order of things" established with the founding of the Republic and reverting to the militarism and oppression characteristic of the old world.

Magan saw himself in a role similar to that of biblical prophets sent to warn kings and nations about the consequences of departure from the divine intention. In this sense, he believed, "ambassadors of Jesus Christ" should make their voices heard "in the courts and congresses of human powers, of earthly governments." And he called upon all citizens of the coming kingdom of God to be true to principle "in things national as well as personal" and to "work for right principles while it is day."

Adventists, in this period, were not hesitant to apply their apocalyptic world view to the foreign policy of their own government, and in so doing to hold the government to its own highest standards of human rights.

Just over a decade later, an arms race contributed to an orgy of blood-letting between the tribes of Europe—primitive in its impulses, but sophisticated in its techniques. With World War I, the century of genocide and WMD had begun.

Attempting to repair the damage, the leading powers met in 1921 for the conference on naval disarmament, convened in Washington by the Harding administration. This endeavor to do the things that make for peace elicited considerable and largely favorable comment from Adventist leaders, not the sort of fatalism and suspicion some might expect to see.[19]

From the annual council in Minneapolis, the church's leaders sent an address to the President, praising him for holding the conference and pronouncing that Adventists "strongly favor a limitation of armaments." They declared that they were "forced to this view by the very logic of our belief in Him who is the Prince of Peace, and of our experience as subjects of His kingdom." The address balanced realism about the elimination of war as long as human beings are sinful with hope that change for the better is possible.

> We are well aware that as war springs from the selfishness of men, the perfect ideal of abiding peace can never be realized in this present world.... But while we may not hope to realize the full fruition of our strivings, the mitigation of the evils of war in any measure is well worth the effort, and should have the consistent support of every lover of peace.

> We are therefore encouraging our people devoutly to pray...for the guidance of those assembled...and that the vast sums spent for armaments of war may be devoted to the amelioration of human woe and the advancement of peaceful pursuits.

On this issue, furthermore, it appears that Adventists did not shy away from acting "in common with other religious bodies."[20]

Nurturing *Shalom*

Peace in the biblical sense of *shalom* also encompasses the full range of human well-being. Peacemaking thus means nurturing *shalom* — restoring health and wholeness in human communities at every level. The major Adventist category here would be health reform, which connects embodied life in all its aspects with the plan of redemption.

One finds a particular abundance of examples, once again, during the 1890s and first decade of the 1900s — political action for prohibition, the multifaceted humanitarian mission to

Chicago led by John Harvey Kellogg and David Paulson, the church's entire medical missionary enterprise spreading throughout the globe. I will elaborate on just one episode, in which we see Adventists nurturing *shalom* amongst a sector of American society subjected to centuries-long, systematic oppression.

After some brief glimmers of hope during the Reconstruction period, racial repression in America was, by the 1890s, rapidly hardening into a comprehensive, legally-entrenched social system. The fourteenth (1868) and fifteenth (1870) amendments to the Constitution had appeared to seal the nation's promise of fully equal citizenship for the freed slaves.

However, as Ellen White pointed out, the nation had failed to seize the opportune moment just after Emancipation to make good on the promise by using money "freely" for the education and economic empowerment of a people still shackled by the legacy of slavery. The government, she wrote, "after a little effort, left the Negro to struggle, unaided…." The endeavors of various Christian agencies, while often noble and courageous, had been far from adequate to meet the need, and Seventh-day Adventist Church had quite simply "failed to act its part."[21]

By the mid-1890s, a national "capitulation to racism"[22] was in full sway, during which segregation and inequality was deeply embedded in the legal and social systems of the Southern states, and in less explicit but nonetheless real ways in American culture as a whole. The Adventist prophet, though, urged her people to defy the prevailing currents with what amounted to a multi-faceted mission for black liberation.[23]

> Walls of separation have been built up between the whites and the blacks. These walls of prejudice will tumble down of themselves as did the walls of Jericho, when Christians obey the Word of God, which enjoins on them supreme love to their Maker and impartial love to their neighbors. For Christ's sake, let us do something now…

That "something" meant building the structures of *shalom* — education and economic opportunity:

The neglect of the colored race by the American nation is charged against them. Those who claim to be Christians have a work to do in teaching them to read and to follow various trades and engage in different business enterprises.[24]

At the very time much of the white South was becoming increasingly intentional about restricting black employment to sharecropping or some other form of perpetual debt peonage, Ellen White insisted that the cotton field *not* be

the only source for a livelihood to the colored people. There will be awakened in them the thought that they are of value with God, and that they are esteemed as His property. The work pointed out is a most needful missionary enterprise. It is the best restitution that can be made to those who have been robbed of their time and deprived of their education.

This mission required a cadre of farmers, financiers, builders, and craftsmen to join ministers and teachers in removing the shackles restricting southern blacks to poverty and a minimal, inferior education at best.[25]

The church never rose as fully to this challenge as Mrs. White had hoped. Yet many of both races, including her son Edson, undertook courageous ventures — risking the violent reaction of white supremacists — in order to nurture *shalom* in all its dimensions. By 1909 results could be seen in 55 primary schools with 1800 pupils in ten southern states, medical facilities in Atlanta and Nashville, the establishment of Oakwood Industrial School, and a modest but solid foundation for an Adventist presence in Black America, consisting of 900 members where there had been less than 50 in 1894.[26]

Subsequently, Adventists seem to have lost much of the vision for being agents of *shalom* for the oppressed. The church fixated on the prophetess's recommendations for temporary accommodation of the social customs of segregation. These controversial counsels reflected her desire that the Adventist assault on the sins of racism and oppression not be violent, suicidal, or noisy. The difficult issues raised by her counsel on accommodation cannot be brushed aside, but they also cannot be understood apart from their context in the saga of a radical mission to build *shalom* in the midst of pervasive bigotry and brutality.

Decades later, Martin Luther King, Jr. would credit the social gospel theologian Walter Rauschenbusch for one of the key insights shaping King's philosophy of nonviolent social change: that the gospel "deals with the whole man—not only his soul but his body, not only his spiritual well-being but his material well-being."[27] That these famous Baptists developed a basic Adventist principle in ways that Adventists largely failed to for much of the twentieth century does not make it any less integral to the Adventist heritage.

Indeed, we owe much gratitude to Roy Branson, E.E. Cleveland, Charles Scriven, Charles Teel and the others who, since the 1960s, have stirred renewed awareness about what the faithful practice of Adventism means in the public arena.

Now we must ask ourselves, Do we want to build on the momentum they generated? In a new era of reconfigured and intensified worship of war-making, what will we do with Adventism's peacemaking heritage? To borrow a phrase from James White, How interested are we, during our own time of perilous conflict, in marching with the ranks of those "who have enlisted to serve under the prince of peace"?[28]

9

Historic Documents

I

A War for Slavery

Excerpt from "OPENING HEAVENS, SEVENTH-DAY   1846
SABBATH, AND WAYMARKS"
by Joseph Bates

Note: *Bates here comments on the celebration of U.S. victories in the war with Mexico (1846-1848) and the war's significance for the extension of slavery.   This excerpt is included in the booklet* Compilation or Extracts from the Publications of Seventh-day Adventists, Setting Forth their Views of the Sinfulness of War *(Battle Creek, Mich: Seventh-day Adventist Publishing Association, 1865) [Document File 320, Ellen White Estate, Silver Spring, MD].*

What mean these illuminated cities, roaring of cannon, and pealing of bells, and exulting through the land? Is it because Christ is coming to set up his everlasting kingdom here? Oh no. It is the nation's *te deum* in honor of the mighty victory obtained by our gallant murderers (for they would be considered such in *every case*, until they were licensed by the rulers, chosen by the people). What have they done? Why they have killed or murdered thousands more of their neighbors than they have murdered of their own. They have desolated their country for 1200 miles, dispersing their neighbors into caverns, forests and mountains, and in the last great victory they have taken their citadel and fort, and murdered some say from 1000 to 500, mostly women and children; and then let loose between three and four thousand of their enemies famished and starving murderers, that by last accounts were ravaging, pillaging, and devastating all that is pleasant to the eye before them. And they say the whole nation is in a state of anarchy, confusion distress and revolution! What caused this mighty uproar? Why out of about 7,000,000 slaves in the Christian world we of this continent can boast of having about 6,000,000 of them. Our neighbors, the Mexicans, undertook some years ago to obey God by breaking the yoke of their slaves. This was too much for the most enlightened nation under the sun to bear. So a revolt ensued, and finally we took a part of their territory from them; from hence has come this havoc and murder. And one portion of the professed church in this boasted land of Bibles and converts have held a convention, and in their zeal for God, (as they would have it,) have chosen the chief murderer, with some of his principle associates, and made them honorary members of the Methodist Missionary Society during their lives.

II
Why Seventh-day Adventists Cannot Engage in War

ADVENT REVIEW AND SABBATH HERALD   March 7, 1865
by George W. Amadon

1. They could not keep the Lord's holy Sabbath. "The *seventh day* is the Sabbath of the Lord thy God; in it *thou shalt not do any work*." Ex. xx,10. Fighting, as military men tell us, is the hardest kind of work; and the *seventh* day of all days would be the least regarded in the camp and field.
2. The sixth command of God's moral law reads, "Thou shalt not kill." To kill is to take life. The soldier by profession is a practical violater of this precept. But if we would enter into life we must "*keep*" the commandments." Matt. xix,17.
3. "God has called *us* to peace;" and "the weapons of *our* warfare are not carnal." 1 Cor. vii,15; 2 Cor. x,4. The gospel permits us to use no weapons but "the sword of the Spirit."
4. Our kingdom is not of this world. Said Christ to Pilate, "If my kingdom were of this world *then would* my servants *fight*." John xviii,36. This is most indisputable evidence that Christians have nothing to do with carnal instruments of war.
5. We are commanded to love even our enemies. "But I say unto you," says the Saviour, "Love your enemies, bless them that curse you, do good to them that hate you, and pray for them that despitefully use you and persecute you." Matt. v,44. Do we fulfill this command when we blow out their brains with revolvers, or sever their bodies with sabres? "If any man have not the spirit of

Christ he is none of his." Rom. viii,9.

6. Our work is the same as our Master's, who once said, "The Son of man is not come to destroy men's lives, but to save them." Luke ix,56. If God's Spirit sends us to *save* men, does not *some other* spirit send us to *destroy* them? Let us know what manner of spirit we are of.

7. The New Testament command is, "Resist not evil; but whosoever shall smite thee on the right cheek, turn to him the other also." Matt. vii,59. That is, we *had better* turn the other cheek than to smite them back again. Could this scripture be obeyed on the battle field?

8. Christ said to Peter, as he struck the high priest's servant, "*Put up again thy sword.*" Matt. xxvi,2. If the Saviour commanded the apostle to "put up" the sword, certainly his followers have no right to take it. Then let those who are of the world *fight*, but as for us let us *pray*.

III
General Conference Resolutions

THIRD ANNUAL MEETING   May 17, 1865

RESOLVED, That in our judgment, the act of voting when exercised in behalf of justice, humanity and right, is in itself blameless, and may be at some times highly proper; but that the casting of any vote that shall strengthen the cause of such crimes as intemperance, insurrection, and slavery, we regard as highly criminal in the sight of Heaven. But we would deprecate any participation in the spirit of party strife.

RESOLVED, That we acknowledge the pamphlet entitled 'Extracts From the Publications of Seventh-day Adventists Setting Forth Their Views of the Sinfulness of War,' as a truthful representation of the views held by us from the beginning of our existence as a people, relative to bearing arms.

Our Duty to the Government

RESOLVED, That we recognize civil government as ordained of God, that order, justice, and quiet may be maintained in the land; and that the people of God may lead quiet and peaceable lives in all godliness and honesty. In accordance with this fact we acknowledge the justice of rendering tribute, custom, honor, and reverence to the civil power, as enjoined in the New Testament. While we thus cheerfully render to Caesar the things which the Scriptures show to be his, we are compelled to decline all participation in acts of war and bloodshed as being inconsistent with the duties enjoined upon us by our divine Master toward our enemies and toward all mankind.

FIFTH ANNUAL SESSION   May 14, 1867

RESOLVED, That it is the judgment of this Conference, that the bearing of arms, or engaging in war, is a direct violation of the teachings of our Saviour and the spirit and letter of the law of God. Yet we deem it our duty to yield respect to civil rulers, and obedience to all such laws as do not conflict with the word of God. In the carrying out of this principle we render tribute, customs, reverence, etc.

SIXTH ANNUAL SESSION   May 14, 1868

WHEREAS, In the struggle through which our country lately passed for its national existence, our sympathies were with our rulers and our government in their efforts to maintain law and order; and in view of the unsettled state of our national affairs, and of the troubles lying before us in the future, we shall continue to pray for those in authority, that they may have wisdom to govern with discretion and in the fear of God; and while we cheerfully pay tribute and honor to those to whom they are due, desiring to live peaceable and quiet lives, as law-abiding people,

RESOLVED, That we feel called upon to renew our request to our brethren to abstain from worldly strife of every nature, believing that war was never justifiable except under the immediate direction of God, who of right holds the lives of all creatures in his hand; and that no such circumstance now appearing, we cannot believe it to be right for the servants of Christ to take up arms to destroy the lives of their fellow-men.

IV
The Kingdom of Christ

REVIEW AND HERALD   August 18, 1896
by Mrs. E.G. White

WHEREUNTO shall we liken the kingdom of God?" said Christ, "or with what comparison shall we compare it?" Christ found the kingdoms of the world corrupt. After Satan was expelled from heaven, he erected his standard of rebellion on this earth, and sought by every means to win men to his standard. In order the more successfully to gain the allegiance of the world, he put on the garb of religion. By familiar intercourse, through his agents, with the inhabitants of the world, he worked to extend his power, that the contagion of evil might be wide-spread. His purpose was to establish a kingdom which would be governed by his own laws, and carried on with his own resources, independent of God; and so well did he succeed, that when Christ came to the world to establish a kingdom, he looked upon the governments of men, and said, "Whereunto shall we liken the kingdom of God?" Nothing in civil society afforded him a comparison. The world had cast aside that class of people most needing care and attention; even the most earnest religionists among the Jews, filled with pride and prejudice, neglected the poor and needy, and some among them frowned upon their existence.

In striking contrast to the wrong and oppression so universally practised were the mission and work of Christ. Earthly kingdoms are established and upheld by physical force, but this was not to be the foundation of the Messiah's kingdom.

In the establishment of his government no carnal weapons were to be used, no coercion practised; no attempt would be made to force the consciences of men. These are the principles used by the prince of darkness for the government of his kingdom. His agents are actively at work, seeking in their human independence to enact laws which are in direct contrast to Christ's mercy and loving-kindness.

Prophecy has plainly stated the nature of Christ's kingdom. He planned a government which would use no force; his subjects would know no oppression. The symbols of earthly governments are wild beasts, but in the kingdom of Christ, men are called upon to behold, not a ferocious beast, but the Lamb of God. Not as a fierce tyrant did he come, but as the Son of man; not to conquer the nations by his iron power, but "to preach good tidings unto the meek;" "to bind up the broken-hearted, to proclaim liberty to the captives, and the opening of the prison to them that are bound;" "to comfort all that mourn." He came as the divine Restorer, bringing to oppressed and downtrodden humanity the rich and abundant grace of Heaven, that by the power of his righteousness, man, fallen and degraded though he was, might be a partaker of divinity.

In the eyes of the world, Christ was peculiar in some things. Ever a friend of those who most needed his protection, he comforted the needy, and befriended those shunned by the proud and exclusive Jews. The forsaken ones felt his protection, and the convicted, repentant soul was clothed with his salvation. And he required of his subjects that they give aid and protection to the oppressed. No soul that bears the image of God is to be placed at the footstool of human power. The greatest possible kindness and freedom are to be granted to the purchase of the blood of Christ. Over and over again in his teaching, Christ presented the value of true humility, showing how necessary it is that we exercise helpfulness, compassion, and love toward one another.

Professed Christians of today have the example of Christ before them, but do they follow it? Often, by the hardness of their hearts, they make it manifest that they do not belong to the kingdom of Christ. Too many educate themselves to censure and condemn, repulsing with harsh, stinging words, those who may seek their help. But cold-hearted worldliness excludes the love of Jesus from the heart. We can cooperate with Christ in the upbuilding of his kingdom only by being sanctified by his Spirit. We must use no force, take up no weapons to compel obedience; for to do this would be to exhibit the same spirit revealed by the enemies of Christ.

Christ can do nothing for the recovery of man until, convinced of his own weakness and stripped of all self-sufficiency and pride, he puts himself under the control of God. Then and then only can he be a true subject of God. No confidence can be placed in human greatness, human intellect, or human plans. We must place ourselves under the guidance of an infinite mind, acknowledging that without Jesus we can do nothing. "Humble yourselves in the sight of the Lord, and he shall lift you up." "Do ye think that the Scripture saith in vain, The spirit that dwelleth in us lusteth to envy? But he giveth more grace. Wherefore he saith, God resisteth the proud, but giveth grace unto the humble."

Christ taught that his church is a spiritual kingdom. He himself, "the Prince of peace," is the head of his church. In his person humanity, inhabited by divinity, was represented to the world. The great end of his mission was to be a sin-offering for the world, that by the shedding of blood an atonement might be made for the whole race of men. With a heart ever touched with the feelings of our infirmities, an ear ever open to the cry of suffering humanity, a hand ever ready to save the discouraged and despairing, Jesus, our Saviour, "went about doing good." His words inspired hope; his precepts awakened men to faith, and caused them to put their trust in him.

Before man can belong to the kingdom of Christ, his character must be purified from sin and sanctified by the grace of Christ. He must become a member of Christ's body, receiving nourishment from him as the branches of the vine derive their strength from the parent stalk. And all who are members of the kingdom of Christ will represent him in character and disposition. Who are thus working out their lives in the service of Christ? All such will sit with him on his throne. But all who exalt themselves, all who oppress their fellow men in any wise, do this to Jesus Christ; for every soul has been purchased at an infinite price, and through faith in Christ is capable of receiving immortality, to live through the eternal ages.

How long God will bear with the heartless indifference shown in the treatment of men toward their fellow men, we cannot determine. But "whatsoever a man soweth, that shall he also reap." If men sow deeds of love and compassion, words of comfort, hope, and encouragement, they will reap that which they have sown.

Christ longs to manifest his grace, and stamp his character and image upon the whole world. He was offered the kingdoms of this world by the one who revolted in heaven, to buy his homage to the principles of evil; but he come to establish a kingdom of righteousness, and he would not be bought; he would not abandon his purpose. This earth is his purchased inheritance, and he would have men free and pure and holy. The world's Redeemer hungered and thirsted for sympathy and co-operation; and his earthly pilgrimage of toil and self sacrifice was cheered by the prospect that his longings would be satisfied, that his work would not be for naught. And though Satan works through human instrumentalities to hinder the purpose of Christ, there are triumphs yet to be accomplished through the blood shed for the world, that will bring glory to God and to the Lamb. His kingdom will extend, and embrace the whole world. The heathen will be given for his inheritance, and the uttermost parts of the earth for his possession. Christ will not be satisfied till victory is complete. But "he shall see of the travail of his soul, and shall be satisfied." "So shall they fear the name of the Lord from the west, and his glory from the rising of the sun."

V
"A Novel Christian Duty"

REVIEW AND HERALD   July 12, 1898
Alonzo T. Jones & Uriah Smith   Editors

IN connection with the war that is now being waged with Spain, there is one amusing thing; and that is the efforts of the pulpits and the religious press to make it appear Christian—to make it fit with the sermon on the mount.

Recognizing the Spaniards as their enemies—they *call* them "*our* enemies"—and being forced to recognize that there has been, that there is yet, and that there is likely to be, considerable killing of them, these good "Christian" preachers and editors find considerable difficulty in making all this harmonize with the Lord's direction, "Love your enemies."

The *Independent* maintains that when the war is over, "we" will love the Spaniards just as much as ever, and will do only good to them. But Jesus did not say, When you have killed all the enemies you can kill, then love all the rest. The love of Christ—that love alone which can love enemies—is a love that will not allow us to kill any of them. This love loves them so that it will not do anything that would even lead to the killing of them. Christian love loves *all* enemies long before the war is over, long before those professing it have killed all they can of them; it loves them so that there can be no war against them at all.

A doctor of divinity publishes an article on this subject, under the text, "I say unto you, Love your enemies;" and his first sentence is, "Americans are confronted to-day with an entirely novel Christian duty." And this "novel Christian duty" is the duty of loving their enemies while they are fighting them, and doing everything possible to kill all of them they possibly can! or else it is the duty of fighting and killing all of their enemies they possibly can, while loving them! It is not decidedly clear which. However, either way, the "duty" is sufficiently novel to deserve notice.

We should say that in either case that *is* decidedly a novel Christian duty—so novel, indeed, that it is difficult to conceive how anybody who understands the first principle of Christianity could ever be "confronted" with it, or think that anybody *could* ever be confronted with it.

This doctor of divinity fears that such a novel situation threatens the "demoralization of our Christian consciousness." But any Christian consciousness that will allow the possessor of it to kill his enemies, even going across seas to hunt them down and kill them—such a Christian consciousness is already absolutely demoralized.

Again, he says: "To love our 'enemies' is intelligently and actively to pity them. This we do. What American would stay his hand from ministering to the man wounded and suffering, because he is a Spaniard! Rather, we would help him the more promptly and joyfully. This much of Christ's spirit we have thoroughly learned. There is no fear that Spanish prisoners of war will be starved or harshly treated, or even taunted."

What a beautifully active Christian pity that is, indeed, that will allow the possessor of it to do his best to kill an "enemy," and having succeeded in only wounding him, and so causing him to suffer, *then* stays not the hand from ministering to him! *only* then becomes at all active!

But the true question here is not, "What American would stay his hand from ministering to a man wounded and suffering because he is a Spaniard?" but, What Christian would wound a man, and cause him to suffer, and that in a direct effort to kill him because he is a Spaniard, or any other "enemy"?

How much of Christ's spirit has any man even partially, much less "thoroughly," learned who will do everything he can to kill his "enemies," and will wound and make prisoners of war all that he can not kill? We were *Christ's* enemies; and instead of doing his best to kill us, he suffered us to kill him. We were enemies, but instead of wounding us, "he was wounded for our transgressions." We were enemies; but instead of causing us to suffer, he suffered for us; he "endured the cross," "the just for the unjust, that he might bring us to God."

Again, this doctor of divinity says that "Christian love does not demand that we make war feebly." No; Christian love demands that its possessor shall not make war at all. "Put up again thy sword into his place," is the word of the Author of Christianity, the embodiment of Christian love.

So long as men think they can be Christians, and at the same time be a part of worldly governments—a part of nations which do fight and will fight; which do make war, and kill all the enemies they can, and wound and make prisoners of war all the others—just so long will they be confronted with that "novel Christian duty" which is so entirely novel that it works the absolute "demoralization of Christian consciousness" in everyone who occupies such an attitude.

But just as soon as men recognize the truth that Christians are not of this world. but are chosen *out* of the world; that Christians are strangers and pilgrims on the earth, seeking a country, even a heavenly; that no Christian can make war—that no Christian can kill even his enemies, even in war—just so soon will they be easily rid of the inconsistency of the "novel Christian duty" of doing their best to kill the "enemies" whom they "love," and of exercising active Christian pity toward them only when, having failed to kill them, they are wounded and suffering.

When men will hold Christianity as that which separates from this world, and all that is of this world; as that which lifts them above this world, and joins them to heaven; as that which empties men altogether of the Spirit of this world, and fills them with the Spirit of heaven and of God, *then* this world will have a chance to know that God has sent Jesus Christ into the world, and has loved us as he loves Jesus Christ.

VI
Address to President Harding

ANNUAL CONFERENCE — GENERAL CONFERENCE   October
Minneapolis, Minnesota   1921

To His Excellency,
    WARREN G. HARDING,
      President of the United States:

The leading official representatives of the Seventh-day Adventist church in the United States, assembled in annual conference at Minneapolis, Minn., Oct. 12-26, 1921, beg leave to submit to you the following address:

We desire to express to you our hearty accord with the commendable efforts now being put forth under your leadership in behalf of international peace and tranquility. In these days of world-wide distress and confusion, it is most gratifying to hear the voice of our Chief Magistrate striking a clear note of hope and courage, and to witness the exercise of his high office in behalf of international amity and pacification. Civil government is ordained of God (Rom. 13:1). And those occupying positions of authority in the state are justly entitled to that respect and loyalty which belong to those who serve as the "ministers of God" for the proper regulation of social order. This respect and loyalty we sincerely entertain for the head of our great Republic and for those associated with him in the executive, legislative, and judicial branches of our Government.

As Seventh-day Adventists, in common with other religious bodies, we strongly favor a limitation of armaments, and if it were possible in the present state of society, we would favor the abolition of all war among the nations of man. We are forced to this view by the very logic of our belief in Him who is the Prince of Peace, and of our experience as subjects of His kingdom.

Throughout their history, Seventh-day Adventists, in common with other religious bodies, have been consistently and uncompromisingly loyal to the great principles of civil and religious liberty—principles which constitute the very foundation of our Government and the bulwark of our democracy.

Sincerely believing in the words of the Saviour, that they should render "unto Caesar the things which are Caesar's, and unto God the things that are God's," they regard as sacred and inviolable their duty to civil government in every function of its exercise wherein such exercise does not conflict with the plain requirements of the law of God and the principles of the gospel of Jesus Christ.

The understanding of the teachings of the gospel which Seventh-day Adventists entertain, has not permitted them throughout their history as a church in this country to bear arms. They believe that the teachings of Christ are opposed to war, and that their design is to promote peace and good will among all who dwell upon the earth. Seventh-day Adventists, therefore, are noncombatant in faith and practice. Both in the Civil War and the recent World War, they were recognized by our Government as noncombatants, and were accorded the rights and privileges, exemptions and immunities, which the Government graciously provided for those holding noncombatant views as a matter of conscience. Members of our churches called to service were assigned to noncombatant duty, and in such labor thousands of our young men rendered faithful and loyal service to their country and to their fellow men.

Holding these noncombatant principles, we note with particular interest your successful efforts to secure an international conference for the discussion of the limitation of armaments. We heartily commend the wise statesmanship and humane sentiment which prompted this laudable action. We are well aware that as war springs from the selfishness of men, the perfect ideal of abiding peace can never be realized in this present world. Only as the hearts of individual men and women

106

are changed by Christ's grace, will the nations of earth submit to the principles of right and righteousness. But while we may not hope to realize the full fruition of our strivings, the mitigation of the evils of war in any measure is well worth the effort, and should have the consistent support of every lover of peace. We are therefore encouraging our people devoutly to pray for your personal guidance, and for the guidance of those assembled in the Conference for the Limitations of Armaments, that the great Ruler of nations may further the cause of international peace, to the end that future war and bloodshed, with all their attendant and consequent horrors, may be averted, and that the vast sums spent for armaments of war may be devoted to the amelioration of human woe and to the advancement of peaceful pursuits.

A.G. DANIELLS, *President.*
W.T. KNOX, *Treasurer.*
J.L. SHAW, *Secretary.*

Published in the Review and Herald *(8 December 1921): 2.*

VII
Statement on Peace

GENERAL CONFERENCE SESSION   June 27, 1985
Neal C. Wilson, *President*

One of the great political and ethical issues of our day is the question of war and peace. It is both complicated and convoluted. Despair hovers around hearts and minds, for millions expect a nuclear holocaust without the basic hope of afterlife or eternal life.

Today there is a new situation, unparalled in history. Human beings have developed the means of humanity's own destruction, means that are becoming more and more "effective" and "perfected" — although these are hardly the right words. Since World War II, civilians are no longer just occasionally or incidentally harmed; they have become the target.

Christians believe that war is the result of sin. Since the Fall of man, strife has been a perennial fact of human existence. "Satan delights in war.... It is his object to incite nations to war against one another." — *The Great Controversy*, p. 589. It is a diversionary tactic to interfere with the gospel task. While global conflict has been prevented during the past forty years, there have been perhaps 150 wars between nations and within nations, with millions perishing in these conflicts.

Today virtually every government claims it is working for disarmament and peace. Often the known facts appear to point in a different direction. Nations spend a huge portion of their financial resources to stockpile nuclear and other war materials, sufficient to destroy civilization as it is known today. News reports focus on the millions of men and women and children who suffer and die in wars and civil unrest and have to live in squalor and poverty. The arms race, with its colossal waste of human funds and resources, is one of the most obvious obscenities of our day.

It is therefore right and proper for Christians to promote peace. The Seventh-day Adventist Church urges every nation to "beat its swords into plowshares" and its "spears into pruning hooks" (Isa. 2:4). The church's Bible-based Fundamental Belief No. 7 states that men and women were "created for the glory of God" and were "called to love Him and one another, and to care for their environment," not to destroy or hurt one another. Christ Himself said, "Blessed are the peacemakers: for they shall be called the children of God" (Matt. 5:9).

While peace cannot be found in official church pronouncements, the authentic Christian church is to work for peace between the first and second advents of Christ. However, hope in the Second Coming must not live in a social vacuum. The Adventist hope must manifest and translate itself into deep concern for the well-being of every member of the human family. True, Christian action today and tomorrow will not of itself usher in the coming kingdom of peace; God alone brings this kingdom by the return of His son. In a world filled with hate and struggle, a world of ideological strife and of military conflicts, Seventh-day Adventists desire to be known as peacemakers and work for worldwide justice and peace under Christ as the head of a new humanity.

VIII
A Seventh-day Adventist Call for Peace

GENERAL CONFERENCE EXECUTIVE   April 18, 2002
COMMITTEE – Spring Meeting

WE ARE LIVING in an increasingly unstable and dangerous world. Recent events have resulted in a heightened sense of vulnerability and personal or corporate fear of violence. Throughout the world, countless millions are haunted by war and apprehension and are oppressed by hate and intimidation

Total War

Humanity has, since the middle of the last century, been living in an age of total war. Total war implies the theoretical possibility that, except for the providence of God, earth's inhabitants could wipe out their entire civilization. Nuclear weapons and biochemical arms of mass destruction are aimed at centers of population. Whole nations and societies are mobilized or targeted for war, and when such war erupts it is carried on with the greatest violence and destruction. The justification of war has become more complex, even though advances in technology make possible greater precision in destroying targets with a minimum of civilian casualties.

A New Dimension

While both the United Nations and various religious bodies have proclaimed the first decade of the 21st century as a decade for the promotion of peace and security in the place of violence in its various forms, a new and insidious dimension of violence has emerged: organized international terrorism. Terrorism itself is not new, but worldwide terrorist networks are. Another new factor is the appeal to so-called divine mandates as the rationale for terrorist activity under the guise of culture war, or even "religious" war.

The rise of international terrorism makes it clear that it is not only a nation or state that makes war, but human beings in various combinations. As one of the leading founders of the Seventh-day Adventist Church pointed out a century ago, "The inhumanity of man toward man is our greatest sin."[1] Indeed, human nature is prone to violence. From a Christian perspective, all this inhumanity is really part of a cosmic war, the great controversy between good and evil.

Terrorism Exploits the Concept of God

Terrorists, in particular those having motivations based on religion, claim that their cause is absolute and that taking lives indiscriminately is fully justified. While they claim to be representing the justice of God, they wholly fail to represent the great love of God.

Furthermore, such international terrorism is totally at odds with the concept of religious liberty. The former is based on political and/or religious extremism and fundamentalistic fanaticism which arrogate the right to impose a certain religious conviction or worldview and to destroy those who oppose their convictions. Imposing one's religious views on other people, by means of inquisition and terror, involves an endeavor to exploit and manipulate God by turning Him into an idol of evil and violence. The result is a disregard for the dignity of human beings created in the image of God.

While it is inevitable that nations and people will try to defend themselves by responding in a military way to violence and terror—which sometimes results in short-term success—lasting answers to deep problems of division in society cannot be achieved by using violent means.

The Pillars of Peace

From both a Christian and practical perspective, any lasting peace involves at least four ingredients: dialogue, justice, forgiveness, and reconciliation.

Dialogue – There needs to be dialogue and discussion in place of diatribe and the cry for war. Lasting peace does not result from violent means, but is achieved by negotiation, dialogue, and, inevitably, political compromise. In the long run, reasoned discourse has superior authority over military force. In particular, Christians should always be ready to "reason together," as the Bible says.

Justice – Unfortunately, the world is rampant with injustice and a fallout of injustice is strife. Justice and peace join hands, as do injustice and war. Poverty and exploitation breed discontent and hopelessness, which lead to desperation and violence.

On the other hand, "God's word sanctions no policy that will enrich one class by the oppression and suffering of another."[2]

Justice requires respect for human rights, in particular religious liberty which deals with the profoundest human aspirations and undergirds all human rights. Justice requires nondiscrimination, respect for human dignity and equality, and a more equitable distribution of the necessities of life. Economic and social policies will either produce peace or discontent. Seventh-day Adventist concern for social justice is expressed through the support and promotion of religious liberty, and through organizations and departments of the Church which work to relieve poverty and conditions of marginalization. Such

111

efforts on the part of the Church can, over time, reduce resentment and terrorism.

Forgiveness – Forgiveness is usually thought of as necessary to heal broken interpersonal relationships. It is highlighted in the prayer Jesus asked His followers to pray (Matt. 6:12). However, we must not overlook the corporate, societal, and even international dimensions. If there is to be peace, it is vital to drop the burdens of the past, to move beyond well-worn battle grounds, and to work toward reconciliation. At a minimum, this requires overlooking past injustices and violence; and, at its best, it involves forgiveness which absorbs the pain without retaliating.

Because of sinful human nature and the resulting violence, some form of forgiveness is necessary in order to break the vicious cycle of resentment, hate, and revenge on all levels. Forgiveness goes against the grain of human nature. It is natural for human beings to deal in terms of revenge and the return of evil for evil.

There is, therefore, first of all the need to foster a culture of forgiveness in the Church. As Christians and church leaders, it is our duty to help individuals and nations to liberate themselves from the shackles of past violence and refuse to reenact year after year, and even generation after generation, the hatred and violence generated by past experiences.

Reconciliation – Forgiveness provides a foundation for reconciliation and the accompanying restoration of relationships that have become estranged and hostile. Reconciliation is the only way to success on the road to cooperation, harmony, and peace.

We call upon Christian churches and leaders to exercise a ministry of reconciliation and act as ambassadors of goodwill, openness, and forgiveness. (See 2 Cor. 5:17-19.) This will always be a difficult, sensitive task. While trying to avoid the many political pitfalls along the way, we must nevertheless proclaim liberty in the land—liberty from persecution, discrimination, abject poverty, and other forms of injustice. It is a Christian responsibility to endeavor to provide protection for those who are in danger of being violated, exploited, and terrorized.

Support of Quality of Life

Silent efforts of religious bodies and individuals behind the scenes are invaluable. But this is not enough: "We are not just creatures of a spiritual environment. We are actively interested in everything that shapes the way we live and we are concerned about the well-being of our planet." The Christian ministry of reconciliation will and must "contribute to the restoration of human dignity, equality, and unity through the grace of God in which human beings see each other as members of the family of God."[3]

Churches should not only be known for spiritual contributions—though these are foundational—but also for their support of quality of life, and in this connection peacemaking is essential. We need to repent from expressions or deeds of violence that Christians and churches, throughout history and even more recently, have either been involved in as actors, have tolerated, or have tried to justify. We appeal to Christians and people of good will all around the world to take an active role in making and sustaining peace, thus being part of the solution rather than part of the problem.

Peacemakers

The Seventh-day Adventist Church wishes to stand for the uncoercive harmony of God's coming kingdom. This requires bridge-building to promote reconciliation between the various sides in a conflict. In the words of the prophet Isaiah, "You will be called the repairer of the breach, the restorer of the streets in which to dwell" (Isa. 58:12). Jesus Christ, the Prince of Peace, wants His followers to be peacemakers in society and hence calls them blessed (Matt. 5:9).

Culture of Peace Through Education

The Seventh-day Adventist Church operates what may be the second largest worldwide parochial school system. Each of its more than 6,000 schools, colleges, and universities is being asked to set aside one week each school year to emphasize and highlight, through various programs, respect, cultural awareness, nonviolence, peacemaking, conflict resolution, and reconciliation as a way of making a specifically "Adventist" contribution to a culture of social harmony and peace. With this in mind, the Church's Education Department is preparing curricula and other materials to help in implementing this peace program.

The education of the church member in the pew, for nonviolence, peace, and reconciliation, needs to be an ongoing process. Pastors are being asked to use their pulpits to proclaim the gospel of peace, forgiveness, and reconciliation which dissolves barriers created by race, ethnicity, nationality, gender, and religion, and promotes peaceful human relations between individuals, groups, and nations.

The Christian Hope

While peacemaking may seem to be a forbidding task, there is the promise and possibility of transformation through renewal. All violence and terrorism are really one aspect of the ongoing controversy, in theological terms, between Christ and Satan. The Christian has hope because of the assurance that evil—the mystery of iniquity—will run its course and be conquered by the Prince of Peace and the world will be made new. This is our hope.

The Old Testament, despite the record of wars and violence, looks forward to the new creation and promises, like the New Testament, the end of the vicious cycle of war and terror, when arms will disappear and become agricultural implements, and peace and knowledge of God and His love will cover the whole world like the waters cover the oceans. (See Isa. 2:4, 11:9.)

In the meantime, we need, in all relationships, to follow the golden rule, which asks us to do unto others as we would wish them to do unto us (see Matt. 7:12), and not only love God, but love as God loves. (See 1 John 3:14, 15; 4:11, 20, 21.)

1. Ellen G. White, *Ministry of Healing*, p. 163.
2. Ibid, p. 187.
3. Quote from Pastor Jan Paulsen, President of the General Conference of Seventh-day Adventists.

10
The Adventist Peace Fellowship
Becoming God's Partners in Peacemaking

Origins

The Adventist Peace Fellowship (APF) emerged out of informal discussions during 2001 among Adventists in Takoma Park, Maryland, who wished to explore and act on the meaning of Christian discipleship and the Seventh-day Adventist heritage for peacemaking in a world rent by violence.

Since then it has been welcomed with enthusiasm by hundreds of supporters throughout the world.

Mission

Our mission is to:

* advance understanding of the significance for peacemaking of the beliefs and heritage of the Adventist movement;
* facilitate cooperative action on current issues;
* link Adventists with resources, people, and organizations dedicated to peacemaking.

Vision

SEVENTH-DAY ADVENTISTS UNDERSTAND themselves to be a people with a unique mission in history, charged with carrying the Gospel of Christ around the world and living as faithful witnesses to the commandments and call of God. From its earliest roots, this has meant that Adventists are a people concerned with restoring personal and social wholeness through a commitment to justice and peace. We remember the Sabbath day not only as a memorial of creation, but also as a symbol of divine justice in the face of political and economic oppression. We hold fast to the faith of Jesus not only by proclaiming his Advent, but by refusing violence and coercion as tools to establish God's kingdom. The radical witness of the Adventist pioneers—who decried slavery, championed religious liberty, agitated against American imperialism, and refused to bear arms in the military—stands as a testament to these convictions. Yet too often we have lost sight of the prophetic social and ethical vision of our founders and Founder. Instead of challenging society as radical witnesses for peace, we have often uncritically accepted its assumptions and moral reasoning. Alternatively, we have at times withdrawn from the work of peace into spiritual and communal isolation. Both impulses, it is clear, can only be fatal to our calling and commission.

WE THEREFORE APPEAL TO ALL ADVENTISTS, as fellow disciples and followers of Christ, to join us in reclaiming our church's historic commitment to social action and radical dissent. We urge all Adventists to re-covenant to obey the high ethical call of the center cross: the call to active, nonviolent resistance to evil. And we challenge all Adventists to engage in the vital work of restoring community through active service to society.

Covenant
The Adventist Peace Fellowship is a covenant of word and action. We seek to foster harmony and justice in our diverse lands, communities, homes and lives by:

1. Studying and proclaiming the Hebrew understanding of shalom and Christ's teaching concerning nonviolence;
2. Reclaiming Adventism's historic vision for personal and social peace, including its commitment to: nonviolence, economic justice, care for creation, and freedom of conscience;
3. Dialoging with persons of other faiths who are equally

concerned with the cause of peace;

4. Engaging in acts of voluntary service within our local communities;

5. Building communities that transcend racial, cultural, national, and economic differences;

6. Supporting persons around the world whose commitment to peace entails severe hardship and physical peril;

7. Urging a stronger commitment to social activism among all Adventists, at all church and institutional levels.

To Join

If you are attracted by this vision and in harmony with the commitments expressed in the "covenant," consider joining APF. Information on doing so is at www.adventistpeace.org. Simply putting your name on record is a valuable, practical action on behalf of peace.

Peace Messenger

Anyone who contacts APF may receive a subscription, free of charge, to the e-mail newsletter, the *Peace Messenger*. It offers:

- brief perspectives on current events and issues pertinent to the APF vision and covenant;
- information about what other Adventists are saying and doing about peacemaking;
- selected passages from prophetic voices for peace and justice—past and present.

Contact

ADVENTIST PEACE FELLOWSHIP
P.O. Box 2840
Silver Spring, MD 20915
www.adventistpeace.org
adventistpeace@comcast.net

End Notes

Chapter 1: A Peacemaking Remnant

1. From Psalm 34:11-14, attributed to David. Scriptural citations are from the New Revised Standard Version.
2. Matthew 5:9.
3. G. H. C. Macgregor, *The New Testament Basis of Pacifism* (New York: The Fellowship of Reconciliation, 1936), pp. 82, 83.
4. These points, commonplace in the church's conventional eschatological writing, come through, e.g., in Raymond F. Cottrell, "The Eschaton: A Seventh-day Adventist Perspective of the Second Coming," in *Spectrum* 5 (Winter 1973): 7-31. Although Cottrell alludes helpfully to Matthew 25, on which more later, the overall picture he presents is that of a last-day church helpless against the drift of history and, except for its proclamation, disengaged from the surrounding culture. Concerning the tendency for church eschatologists to condense, or effectively condense, Adventist mission into the expression of warnings, neglected truths, special messages and the like, see the more or less official essay, "Who Constitutes the 'Remnant Church'?" in *Seventh-day Adventists Answer Questions on Doctrine* (Washington, D.C.: Review and Herald, 1957):186-196; see, too, the same tendency in Raoul Dederen's attempt to explain Adventism to a non-Adventist, scholarly readership, "An Adventist Response to 'The Seventh-day Adventists and the Ecumenical Movement," in *The Journal of Ecumenical Studies* 7 (Summer 1970): 558-563, reprinted in *Spectrum* 2 (Autumn 1970): 19-25. For another example, see, in *Adventist Review*, December 2, 1976, pp. 14, 15, the 1976 Annual Council document, "Evangelism and Finishing God's Work," which declared the church's "singular objective" to be proclamation of its special message. For a recent example, see Robert S. Folkenberg, "The Remnant," *Adventist Review*, August 1998, p. 27, where the author declares that the "focal point of the remnant is that it has a unique message...."
5. Norman Gulley, *Christ is Coming* (Hagerstown, MD: Review and Herald Publishing Association, 1998.) These endorsements appear on pp. 3, 5 and 9.
6. For remarks in *Christ is Coming* on Christ's centrality, see, e.g., pp. 52, 140, 358; on history as conflict, see pp. 41, 54; on liberal devaluation of eschatology, see p. 246; on survival of the fittest, see p. 408; on suspicion of empires, see p. 243; on church-state alliances, see pp. 211, 443, 472, 478, 487, 493; on charting, see pp. 507-509. It's fair to say that Gulley does not fully overcome the Adventist preoccupation with

detail. One of his sentences, on p. 509, reads: "As Ussher's chronology is four years off, 1998 is nearly 2002."

7. Ibid., p. 366.

8. Malcolm Bull and Keith Lockhart, in their *Seeking a Sanctuary: Seventh-day Adventism and the American Dream* (San Francisco: Harper & Row, 1989), suggest on p.160 that Adventists are suspicious of all that is "extended in space, what is purely material or animal...." Jesus affirmed space as well as time.

9. On Jesus and creation, see, e.g., Mark 10:6, Matthew 5:45 and 25:14-30; for his sense of Hebrew lineage, see, e.g., Matthew 22:29-40; on his eschatology, see, e.g., Mark 1:15, Luke 17:20,21, and, with a view especially to taking responsibility on earth, Matthew 24 and 25. Many scholars notice that Jesus' Kingdom metaphor is political in connotation. Geza Vermes, on p. 121 of *The Religion of Jesus the Jew* (Minneapolis: Fortress Press, 1993), calls it "essentially political."

10. Robert E. Webber and Rodney Clapp, on p. 122 of *People of the Truth: A Christian Challenge to Contemporary Culture* (Harrisburg, PA: Morehouse Publishing, 1993; originally Harper & Row, 1988), describe the "eschatological community" as having its "eyes on the end," that is, on Jesus Christ, and as living "in the light of this ending, the true ending of the world."

11. For sample backing from Scripture, see John 1 and 10.

12. Gulley, Ibid., pp. 539, 540.

13. Revelation 14:7. The passage starting with verse 6 and proceeding to verse 12 is the scriptural centerpiece of eschatological self-understanding for Adventists. On what it means to affirm that God is creator, see, e.g., Genesis 1 and 2; in particular, see 1:26, 27 (humankind as in the "image of God"), 1:31 (God's creation as "very good") and 2:15-20 (humankind as God's agent in the creation of culture).

14. See Gulley, Ibid., p. 250 for his remarks on the Kingdom, social change and the political arena; p. 539 for the perspective on "human improvement," and p. 441 for the claim that according to the bible the world is getting "worse." My position would be that according to the Bible Kingdom-building, in which we participate as Christ's ambassadors and body (2 Corinthians 5:20 and 2 Corinthians 12:27), is difficult, yet by no means destined to fail at every point; the Second Coming is the *completion* of God's work, not just the interruption of the devil's. See my comment on p. 10 below.

15. Ibid., p. 54. Cf. this remark of Loma Linda University theologian Gerald Winslow: "Certain of their faith in the resurrection of Jesus Christ, [Christians] know that history is not a closed deterministic system but is open to the transforming power of God," in his essay, "Millenium," in Charles Teel, Jr., ed., *Remnant and Republic* (Loma

Linda, CA: Loma Linda University Center for Christian Bioethics, 1995), p. 173.

16. Ellen G. White writes that the "Redeemer" enlists us as "co-workers," and speaks of our "agency" and "co-operation"as "co-workers" in "the cause of God," in *Testimonies for the Church*, 9 vols. (Mountain View: Pacific Press, 1948) 3:382, 391. Cf. her paragraph on the honor of being "co-laborers with Jesus," in which she declares that there is "no limit to the good you may do," in *Messages to Young People* (Nashville, TN: Southern Publishing Association, 1930), p. 125.

17. See my (pompously titled) "The Real Truth About the Remnant," *Spectrum* 17 (October 1986): 6-13 for background on this motif in Adventism, and also for an effort to expand conventional awareness by examining the whole Bible's use of the motif. For this latter, I rely heavily on Gerhard Hasel, *The Remnant* (Berrien Springs, MI: Andrews University Press, 1972, what is a fine book-length treatment of the subject. For further, unconventional reflection on Adventist application of the motif, see Jack W. Provonsha, *A Remnant in Crisis* (Hagerstown, MD: Review and Herald, 1993), as well as a review of that book by James J. Londis, "*Remnant and Crisis* and a Second Disappointment," in *Spectrum* 24 (April 1995): 9-16. Conventional Adventist awareness focuses more or less exclusively on the account in the book of Revelation. Here the Remnant, after Revelation 12:17 and 14:12, comprises all who keep the commandments of God and have the faith of Jesus; in particular, they keep (unlike other Christians) the fourth commandment Sabbath, seen, on this view, as the "seal of the living God" (7:2), the sign, especially in thy last days, of loyalty to God.

18. A 1987 survey of 100 Pacific Union Conference pastors (!) revealed that, by a two-to-one margin, they disagreed with the claim the Adventist Church "constitutes God's remnant people," according to the report of Charles Teel, Jr., in his essay "Remnant," in Charles Teel, Jr., ed., *Remnant and Republic* (Loma Linda, CA: Loma Linda University Center for Christian Bioethics, 1995), p. 19. For thoughtful reflection on this matter, see Jack Provonsha, "The Church as Prophetic Minority," in Roy Branson, ed., *Pilgrimage of Hope* (Takoma Park: Association of Adventist Forums, 1986), pp. 98-107.

19. Gulley, Ibid., p. 52.

20. Other Gospel references to the theme include Mark 6:34 and Matthew 18:12-14, which parallels Luke 15:3-7, not to mention the crystallization of this imagery in the Shepherd discourse of John 10:1-21.

21. See Jeremiah 31:7, 10, 23-26 and 31-34.

22. On shepherd imagery and the covenant of peace, see verses 34 and 36. On the cleansing and renewal of hearts, see verses 21-23, and cf. 36:24-26.
23. Cf. Matthew 2:6 with Micah 5:2-5a; Cf. Luke 1:79 with Isaiah 9:2, 6,7. Ben F. Meyer, S. J., argues that the remnant motif belongs to Jesus' consciousness, in his "Jesus and the Remnant of Israel," *Journal of Biblical Literature* 84 (1965): 123-130.
24. See Matthew 28:20 and John 16 and 17, especially 17:21-23. Cf. Romans 8:1-11, where fellowship with the Spirit of God is virtually the same thing as fellowship with (the risen) Christ.
25. For example, Jesus eats with "tax collectors and sinners" (Mark 2:15 and parallels), speaks well of a Samaritan (Luke 10:29-37), learns from a Syro-Phoenician Gentile woman (Mark 7:24-30), imagines, as Isaiah had done, the temple as a house of prayer for all nations (Mark 11:17 and parallels; cf. Isaiah 56:7 and surrounding verses).
26. Luke 9:51, the beginning of Luke's so-called "travel account." The translation is that of Joseph Fitzmyer, in the Anchor Bible.
27. For example stories or sayings on these themes, see the parable of the Father and Two Sons (Luke 15:11-32); the stories of the healing of the crippled woman and of the inclusion of Mary in the circle of disciples (Luke 13:10-17; 10:38-42); the parable of the wicked tenant farmers (20:9-19); Jesus' saying on the signs of the end and his own refusal to be intimidated, even by Herod's death threats (Luke 21; Luke 13:31-33); his entry into Jerusalem on a colt symbolizing peace through nonviolence (Luke 19:28-40; cf. Zechariah 9:9, 10); his prayer for the forgiveness of his crucifiers (Luke 23:34).
28. See Luke19:29-40; cf. Zechariah 9:9,10, and note a nearby allusion, in verse 7, to the remnant; further mentions occur in chapter 8.
29. See Luke 10:1-23.
30. See, before the turn to Jerusalem, 9:18-23; for Jesus' teaching after the turn to Jerusalem, see 14:27, 18:22, 18:35-43, 22:24-27.
31. See again Psalm 34:14 and Luke1:79; the language of the rest of the sentence mirrors that in Revelation 14:12.
32. See Luke 17;20-21; cf. the apocalypse of Luke 21. See his premonition of his passion, expressed first in Luke 9:22 and repeated during the journey to Jerusalem, in 17:25.
33. See the peace motif in Luke 1 and 2; see his words of greeting after the resurrection in Luke 24:36; see again the description of his entrance into Jerusalem in Luke 19:29-40
34. See Luke 17:33 for Jesus' comment on preoccupation with security. For parables about end-time preparation that follow Jesus' word to the "little flock," see Luke 12:35-48.
35. Gulley's words, Ibid., p. 52, as quoted on p. 5 above.
36. Matthew 5:9.

37. Paul Hanson, in his *The People Called: The Growth of Community in the Bible* (San Francisco: Harper & Row, 1986), p. 474, writes that the struggle of the Hebrew prophets to "preserve the integrity of the covenant community within an increasing secular and pluralistic society" gave rise to the view of the "community of faith as a *remnant* within the larger nation."

38. See Genesis 12:1-4.

39. Jack Provonsha (note 18, above) urged the Adventist community to be a "prophetic minority," in his "The Church as Prophetic Minority." The rest of the sentence (note 3, above) quotes the article epigraph from G. H. C. Macgregor.

40. See Erwin Sicher, "Seventh-day Adventist Publications and the Nazi Temptation," *Spectrum* 8 (March 1977): 11-24; and Sharise Esh, "Adventist Tragedy, Heroism in Rwanda," *Spectrum* 24 (October 1994): 3-11; and the cluster of articles on Koresh in *Spectrum* 23 (May 1993): 18-52.

41. On Stahl, see Charles Teel, "The Radical Roots of Peruvian Adventism," *Spectrum* 21 (December 1990): 5-18; on Weidner, see Herbert Ford, *Flee the Captor* (Nashville: Southern Publishing Association, 1966); on Doss, see Booten Herndon, *The Unlikeliest Hero* (Mountain View, CA: Pacific Press, 1967); on Shelkov, see articles in the cluster, "Adventism and the USSR," in *Spectrum* 19 (November, 1988): 25-54; on Suslic, see "Neither Shells Nor Gloom of War Stays Group From Aiding Sarajevo," *The Washington Post*, 24 June 1993, pp. A29, 30.

42. For Adventist reaction to the Spanish-American War, see Doug Morgan, "Apocalyptic Anit-Imperialists," *Spectrum* 22 (January 1993): 20-27. The 1921 letter may be obtained from Bert Haloviak of the Deparment of Archives and Statistics at the Church's world headquarters, 12501 Old Columbia Pike, Silver Spring, MD 20904. The 1985 statement was published in the *Adventist Review*, December 5, 1985, p. 19.

43. See, e.g., John Brunt, *Now and Not Yet* (Washington, D. C.: Review and Herald, 1987); Sakae Kubo, *God Meets Man: A Theology of the Sabbath and the Second Coming* (Nashville, TN: Southern Publishing Association, 1978); Charles W. Teel, Jr., "Growing Up With John's Beasts: A Rite of Passage," *Spectrum* 21 (May 1991): 25-34; Roy Branson, "Social Reform as a Sacrament of the Second Adventist," *Spectrum* 21 (May 1991): 49-59; Gottfried Oosterwal, *Mission: Possible* (Nashville: Southern Publishing Association, 1972); Steven G. Daily, *Seventh-day Adventism for a New Generation* (Riverside: CA: Better Living Publishers, 1992) Zdravko Plantak, *The Silent Church: Human Right and Adventist Social Ethics* (New York: St. Martin's Press, 1998). Cf. the 1970 essay by Reo M. Christenson, "The Church and Public

Policy," in *Spectrum* 2 (Summer 1970): 23-28, which, in peacemaking fashion, called on the church to address problems of racial conflict, poverty, environmental pollution, crime and war.

44. See Micah 2:12, 4:7, 5:7-8,7:18-20.
45. On true worship and true Sabbathkeeping, note the connection between Sabbath and political freedom in the Deuteronomy 5 version of the fourth commandment; see further, e.g., Isaiah 1:13-17 (note the nearby allusion to the remnant in 1:9), Isaiah 58, Amos 8:5 (note that Amos also, in 5:15, alludes to the remnant); consider, too, that when Luke describes Jesus as worshiping on Sabbath according to his "custom" (Luke 4:16-21), Jesus' public utterance involves, in part, words from the aforementioned Isaiah 58. Micah describes the "one who is to rule in Israel" as being the "one of peace," in 5:2-5.
46. Jan Daffern, in "Singing in a Strange Land," reflects movingly on the Adventist experience of disappointment, and notes the openness it can create to "the disappointed outside our community," in Roy Branson, ed., *Pilgrimage of Hope* (Takoma Park: Association of Adventist Forums, 1986), pp. 89-97.
47. T. S. Eliot, *Four Quartets* (New York: Harcourt, Brace & World, 1971), p. 59.

Chapter 2: A People of Prophecy

1. On Seventh-day Adventism's self-understanding as "Prophetic Minority" see Charles Teel, "Withdrawing Sect, Accommodating Church, Prophesying Remnant: Dilemmas in the Institutionalization of Adventism" (unpublished manuscript of the presentation at the 1980 Theological Consultation for Seventh-day Adventist Administrators and Religion Scholars, Loma Linda University, 1980).
2. Enid Mellor, "Reading the Prophets Today", in *Prophets and Poets* (Abingdon, 1997).
3. Walter Brueggemann, *Prophetic Imagination* (Fortress, 1978).
4. For this division into four elements of prophetic ethics I am indebted to Walter Harrelson. See his "Prophetic Ethics", in *A New Dictionary of Christian Ethics* (1986), 508-512.
5. Brueggemann, 33.
6. Brueggemann, 41-42, 44.
7. Summarized in Brueggemann, 44.
8. Jack W. Provonsha, *Remnant in Crisis* (Hagerstown, MD: Review and Herald, 1993), 50.
9. Provonsha, 50-51.
10. See, for example, C. H. Dodd, *Gospel and Law: Bampton Lectures in America* (Cambridge: Cambridge University Press, 1951), 62-63.
11. In *Prophets and Poets* (Abingdon, 1997), 32.

12. Walter Brueggemann, *Isaiah 1-39,* Westminster Bible Companion 1 (Louisville: Westminster John Knox, 1998).
13. Luke 4:18-21. Cf. Karl Barth, *Deliverance to the Captives,* translated by Marguerite Wieser with Preface by John Marsh, (London: SCM Press, 1961).
14. John Brunt, *Now and Not Yet: How Do people Waiting for the Second Coming Respond to Poverty, Lawsuits, Hunger, Political Oppression, Sexuality, and Sin?* (Washington, D. C.: Review and Herald, 1987), 16.
15. Ellen Davis, *Getting Involved with God: Rediscovering the Old Testament.* (Cambridge, Boston, MA: Cowley Publications, 2001), p. 202-208.
16. Davis, 202-208.

Chapter 3: Liberation Theology — The Genuine Article

1. Ellen G. White, *The Great Controversy* (Nampa, ID: Pacific Press Publishing Association, 1911), 577-78.
2. Jeffries M. Hamilton, "The Rest Is Commentary: A Reading of the Ten Commandments," *Quarterly Review* 13 (Fall 1993): 33.
3. Christopher J.H. Wright, "Deuteronomic Depression," *Theology* 19 (Jan. 1994): 33-34.
4. Bruce C. Birch, *Let Justice Roll Down: The Old Testament, Justice, and Christian Life* (Louisville: Westminster John Knox, 1991), 80.
5. Quoted in Elizabeth Isichei, *A History of Christianity in Africa* (Grand Rapids, MI: Eerdmans, 1995), 354.
6. Isichei, 49.
7. Bengt G. Sundkler, *Bantu Prophets in South Africa* (New York: Oxford University Press, 1961), 110.
8. Sundkler, 110.
9. Irving Hexham and Gerhardus C. Oosthuizen, eds., *The Story of Isaiah Shembe,* Hans-Jurgin Becken, trans. (Queenstown, Ontario: Mellon, 1997), 94-95.
10. Joseph B. Danquah, *The Akan Doctrine of God* (London: Lutterworth, 1944), 139.

Chapter 5: God Bless Afghanistan

1. See also Samuel D. Proctor, "A Nation Under God," Walter B. Hoard, ed. *Outstanding Black Sermons, Vol. 2* (Valley Forge: Judson Press, 1979), 89-94.
2. Cited in James H. Cone, *Martin, Malcolm & America* (Maryknoll: Orbis, 1991), 237.
3. 2d ed. (Santa Fe: Bear and Company, 1984)
4. *USA Today* January 25-27, 2002, 7a.
5. *New York Times,* Sunday February 17, 2002, 10.
6. Ellen G. White, *Testimonies* 9:12-13

Chapter 6: Second Advent Hope—the Presence of the Future

1. Excellent resources for further study of the message of Revelation for today in the light of its literary structure and historical context include: Richard Bauckham, *The Theology of the Book of Revelation* (Cambridge University Press: 1993).; Alan A. Boesak, *Comfort and Protest: The Apocalypse from a South African Perspective* (Philadelphia: The Westminster Press, 1987; Eugene H. Peterson, *Reversed Thunder: The Revelation of John & the Praying Imagination* (San Francisco: HarperCollins, 1988); Elisabeth Schüssler Fiorenza *Revelation: Vision of a Just World* (Minneapolis: Augsburg Fortress, 1991).

2. David E. Aune, *Word Biblical Commentary*, ed. Bruce M. Metzger (Dallas, Tex.: Word, 1997), 52a:314-17, identifies sixteen hymnic utterances within the narrative of the book of Revelation: 4:8c, 11; 5:9b-10, 12b, 13b; 7:10b, 12; 11:15b, 17-18; 12:10b-12; 15:3b-4; 16:5b-7b; 19:1b-2, 3, 5b, 6b-8. See also Michael A. Harris, "The Literary Function of Hymns in the Apocalypse of John" (Ph.D. diss., Southern Baptist Theological Seminary, 1989), 4-16.

Chapter 8: Adventism's Peacemaking Heritage

1. Reports on Klimkewicz may be found at the web sites of the Adventist News Network (www.adventist.org), *Spectrum* magazine (www.spectrummagazine.org), and the Adventist Peace Fellowship (www.adventistpeace.org).

2. See "The Peacemaking Remnant: Seven Theses" in the Adventist Voices section at www.adventistpeace.org.

3. See Ronald D. Graybill, "The Abolitionist-Millerite Connection," Ronald L. Numbers and Jonathan M. Butler, eds., *The Disappointed: Millerism and Millenarianism in the Nineteenth Century* (Bloomington: Indiana University Press, 1987), 139-50; and Peter Brock, *Freedom From Violence: Sectarian Nonresistance From the Middle Ages to the Great War* (Toronto: University of Toronto Press, 1991), 230-58.

4. *Testimonies* 1: 264.

5. See his series of three articles collectively entitled "Ellen G. White—Racist or Champion of Equality?," in the *Review and Herald*, April 9, 16, and 23, 1970.

6. D.A. Robinson, A.L. White, and W.C. White, "The Spirit of Prophecy and Military Service," manuscript, 1936, 6-7, Ellen G. White Estate, Silver Spring, MD.

7. Brock provides a thorough analysis of the Civil War-era debate in the Review and Herald over military services in *Freedom From Violence*, 230ff.

8. *Testimonies* 1: 357-361.

9. J. N. Andrews, "Seventh-day Adventists Recognized as Noncombatants," *Review and Herald* 24 (September 13, 1864): 124-25.

10. "Report of the Third Annual Session of the General Conference of Seventh-day Adventists," *Review and Herald* 25 (May 17, 1865): 196-97.

11. General Conference Session Minutes at General Conference Office of Archives and Statistics, http://archives.gc.adventist.org/ast/archives.

12. *The Silent Church: Human Rights and Adventist Social Ethics* (New York: St. Martin's Press, 1998).

13. *A Religious History of the American People* (New Haven: Yale University Press, 1972), 879-80.

14. Cited in Robert Lindner and Richard Pierard, *Twilight of the Saints: Biblical Christianity and Civil Religion in America* (Downers Grove, IL: InterVarsity Press, 1978), 147-48.

15. Ahlstrom, 880.

16. "The Gospel of War," *Review and Herald*, 3 May 1898.

17. "The Present Crisis," supplement to the *Review and Herald*, 3 May 1898.

18. Douglas Morgan, *Adventism and the American Republic: The Public Involvement of a Major Apocalyptic Movement* (Knoxville, TN: University of Tennessee Press, 2001), 66-68.

19. Morgan, 104-06.

20. "Address to President Harding," *Review and Herald*, 8 December 1921: 2.

21. *Testimonies* 9: 205.

22. C. Vann Woodward, *The Strange Career of Jim Crow*, 3rd rev. ed. (New York: Oxford University Press, 1974), pp. 67-109.

23. See Ronald D. Graybill, *Ellen G. White and Church Race Relations* (Washington, D.C.: Review and Herald Publishing Association, 1970) and *Mission to Black America* (Mountain View, CA: Pacific Press Publishing Association, 1971).

24. *The Southern Work*, 44.

25. *The Southern Work*, 51-62.

26. Richard Schwarz and Floyd Greenleaf, *Light Bearers: A History of the Seventh-day Adventist Church*, rev. ed. (Silver Spring, MD: Department of Education, General Conference of Seventh-day Adventists), 234.

27. "Pilgrimage to Nonviolence," *Christian Century*, 13 April 1960.

28. *Review and Herald*, 9 September 1864